A COMMON CALLING

A COMMON CALLING

The Witness of Our Reformation Churches
in North America Today

*The Report of the Lutheran-Reformed Committee
for Theological Conversations, 1988-1992*

Edited by
Keith F. Nickle
Timothy F. Lull

A COMMON CALLING
The Witness of Our Reformation Churches in North America Today

Scripture quotations unless otherwise noted are from the New Revised Standard Version of the Bible, copyright © 1989 by the Division of Christian Education of the National Council of the Churches of Christ in the United States of America.

Cover design: Judy Swanson

Library of Congress Cataloging-in-Publication Data

A common calling : the witness of our reformation churches in North
   America today : the report of the Lutheran-Reformed Committee for
   Theological Conversations, 1988-1992 / edited by Keith F. Nickle,
   Timothy F. Lull.
       p.   cm.
   Includes bibliographical references.
   ISBN 0-8066-2665-8 (alk. paper) :
   1. Lutheran Church—Relations—Reformed Church.   2. Reformed
Church—Relations—Lutheran Church.   I. Nickle, Keith Fullerton,
1933-   II. Lull, Timothy F.   III. Lutheran Reformed Committee
for Theological Conversations.
BX8063.7.R4C66   1993
280'.042—dc20   92-43096
                                                                 CIP

The paper in this publication meets the minimum requirements of American National Standard for Information Sciences—Permanence of Paper for Printed Library Materials, ANSI Z329.48-1984. ∞™

Manufactured in U.S.A.   AF 9-2665

97   96   95   94   93   1   2   3   4   5   6   7   8   9   10

Contents

Preface

The typical reader of this report may feel that she or he has seen it all before. After all, there have been so many ecumenical statements, including several from U.S. Lutheran and Reformed churches. What is there to add from yet another round of dialogue?

If you approach this report in that spirit, you are understandably likely to turn first to our recommendations. We hope you will read and consider them—either first or after you study the rest of the report. But we want you to know that these recommendations emerged out of a complex process of theological conversation and discovery which we have tried to recapture in the body of this report. While this is one more attempt to propose a basis for fellowship among several of these churches, it also provides a different model for future work.

Walk with us through the review of this history and the summary of current positions. In part we have borrowed from the Leuenberg Agreement, which has long served as the basis for recognition and continuing dialogue among European Reformed and Lutheran churches and which we find partly applicable to our situation. But in part we believe that we have learned from the success and the failure of the earlier dialogues. That there is a considerable basis of common commitment, even on the issues that were divisive at the time of the Reformation, seems well established. But what to do about the differences that remain? How much fellowship, if any, is warranted among us?

Our proposal suggests, in the light of our considerable degree of common understanding—on both the basic shape of the Christian faith and on our assigned topics of Predestination, Christology, and the Lord's Supper—that the basis exists for substantial fellowship among these churches. We have taken the term "full communion" from the documents of the ELCA as a term that we believe well describes what we have accomplished and what we propose.

But the "Common Calling" of our title is not simply to get about the task of mutual recognition, nor to let bygones be bygones. We are suggesting that continuing differences, while not an obstacle to the kind of recognition, exchange, and sacramental hospitality that go with "full communion," are in fact the basis for ongoing mutual theological work. Such dialogue would not be seen as a prelude to some future fellowship, but as a necessary and happy part of the mutually complimentary nature of these two traditions. Moreover, we want to capture a sense of mission urgency which we think confronts all four of our churches at this time and in this culture.

Our goal is not to homogenize, but to recognize. Our conclusion is that we have enough agreement to share, not that we are or will soon become theologically identical. Our hope is that readers will study this report, share some of the excitement of mutual discovery which we have experienced, test the validity of our conclusions, and then consider whether it is possible to support this model for our future work.

Keith F. Nickle, Dean
Pittsburgh Theological Seminary
Reformed Co-Chair

Timothy F. Lull, Dean
Pacific Lutheran Seminary
Lutheran Co-Chair

1

Introduction

The present document grew out of unfinished business which was a legacy to the Evangelical Lutheran Church in America and its Reformed partner churches. The story of Reformed-Lutheran relations in the United States has been marked at some times and in some places by division, polemics, and suspicion, but it has held out also the constant promise of unity, cooperation, and mutual understanding based on the common heritage of the Reformation of the sixteenth century. The members of these Conversations are persuaded that this promise can be fulfilled today as we recognize a common calling for the witness of our churches in North America. We are proposing a model of confessional hermeneutics which does not surrender the deep convictions held by our communities of faith but allows for a new relationship that leaves behind the bitterness of the past. Examining in some depth such major theological topics as the Lord's Supper, christology, predestination, and the condemnations of the sixteenth century, we discovered that it was possible to develop fresh lines of thinking about the doctrinal differences between our churches which may change ecumenical relationships in a decisive way. Our hope is that this report finds open hearts and minds and will prepare the way into a common future marked by faithfulness to our common heritage and to our mutual responsibility before the one Lord of the church.

A. The Present Round of Conversations

Official conversations between representatives of Reformed and Lutheran churches in the USA have been held since 1962. The first round of such official dialogue occurred in 1962-1966 under the sponsorship of the North American Area of the World Alliance of Reformed Churches (WARC) and the USA National Committee of the Lutheran World Federation (LWF). Its results were published in the volume *Marburg Revisited* (Augsburg, 1966), which presented the various papers discussed at the meetings, summary statements on each of the doctrinal topics covered, supplementary statements formulated at an evaluation session, and a "Report to the Sponsoring Confessional Organizations."[1] The "Report" concluded:

> As a result of our studies and discussions we see no insuperable obstacles to pulpit and altar fellowship and, therefore, we recommend to our parent bodies that they encourage their constituent churches to enter into discussions looking forward to intercommunion and the fuller recognition of one another's ministries (p. 191).

A second round took place in 1972-74. It issued no more than a terse report, with a set of five general recommendations whose scope fell far short of that of the first series and included the suggestion that "if formal declarations of altar fellowship are desired, this question be dealt with on a church body to church body basis" (printed in *An Invitation to Action*, Fortress Press, 1984, p. 58). A third series, under the auspices of the Division of Theological Studies of the Lutheran Council in the USA (LCUSA) and the Caribbean and North American Area Council of the World Alliance of Reformed Churches, was begun in 1981 and concluded in 1983. The resulting volume, *An Invitation to Action*, (Fortress Press, 1984) made available not only the joint statements on justification, the sacrament of the Lord's Supper, and ministry, but also separate reflections on this dialogue by the Lutheran and Reformed participants and an impressive apparatus of notes and documentation.[2] The report included the recommendation that the churches recognize one another "as churches in which the gospel is proclaimed and the sacraments are administered according to the ordinance of Christ," as well as the mutual recognition of ministries and eucharistic celebrations. It also suggested a detailed process of reception of the dialogue's result in the churches.

None of the participating churches took official action on the recommendations of the first two rounds of dialogue. Such actions, however, were forthcoming in response to *An Invitation to Action*, which was widely studied within the sponsoring churches. The highest assemblies of three of the participating Reformed churches involved adopted the recommendations of the third round of dialogue: the Reformed Church in America (RCA) in 1986, the Presbyterian Church USA (PCUSA) the same year, and the United Church of Christ (UCC) in 1989, while the Cumberland Presbyterian Church (CPC) acted in 1984 to approve the report for study. On the Lutheran side, the Association of Evangelical Lutheran Churches (AELC) and the American Lutheran Church (ALC) acted favorably on the recommendations of the report, while the 1986 Biennial Convention of the Lutheran Church America (LCA) adopted a more guarded response, drafted by its Committee on Ecumenical Relations and proposed by its Executive Council, which called for "a new series of Lutheran-Reformed dialogues" which would need "to elaborate the conclusions reached in *An Invitation to Action* and to answer questions that have arisen about it, e.g., the relation between dialogue reports and the governing and liturgical documents of the churches." The question of the confessional nature of the United Church of Christ as a full participant was addressed and examined at a special consultation in October 1987 in New York City.[3]

The occasion for this present round of Conversations was the creation of a new Lutheran church which, on January 1, 1988, replaced the three predecessor bodies, the AELC, the ALC, and the LCA, and took the name of the Evangelical Lutheran Church in America (ELCA). Since not all predecessor bodies had adopted the recommendations of *An Invitation to Action* and endorsed the establishment of full church fellowship among Reformed and Lutheran churches, the question of the existing degree of fellowship and the remaining steps for its full realization needed to be taken up again between the new church and its Reformed partners. The ELCA Constituting Assembly requested the planning of conversations for this purpose through the ELCA Church Council in June of 1987. The Reformed partner churches responded positively to the invitation, and the first meeting was held in the fall of 1988, followed by regular meetings through March 1992.

11

B. The Task

The responsibilities of the present round of Conversations were spelled out by a communique issued jointly by the leaders of the four churches on February 25, 1988. The members of the Conversation group were charged "to explore what next steps need to be taken on the road to fuller fellowship." The ELCA Church Council specified its expectations of the Lutheran participants more precisely, noting at the same time the common goal:

> The Lutherans were mandated to do the work requested by the constituting convention of the Evangelical Lutheran Church in America and specified by action of the Church Council, including a discussion of such theological topics as the Lord's Supper, Christology, predestination, and mutual condemnations.

> The Lutherans were also mandated to propose strategies for further Lutheran-Reformed relations. The mandate of this new series of conversation partners is clearly to assist the churches in developing a faithful and secure basis for fuller levels of fellowship, including sharing at the Lord's table, recognition of members and ministries, and unity in witness. (1989 Churchwide Assembly, ELCA, Reports and Records, vol. 3, p. 834).

In their report to the First Churchwide Assembly of the ELCA in August of 1989, the Lutheran representatives expressed themselves about their hopes for these Conversations as follows:

> Our goal is to achieve the following by the 1991 assembly of the Evangelical Lutheran Church in America:

> —To review the agreements achieved between Lutherans and Reformed in the United States and Europe since World War II and to recommend a secure basis for the removal of the historical condemnations and barriers to fellowship, resulting in fuller levels of fellowship, which include sharing at the Lord's table, recognition of members and ministries, and unity in witness;

> —To identify critical contributions that the Lutheran and Reformed traditions may make together in their witness to the Gospel in this nation and the world, and to recommend further common theological, pastoral, and mission work for the churches;

> —To recommend specific steps to express the measure of mutual recognition that already exists; and

—To recommend a process for future dialogue to strengthen evangelical clarity and mutual accountability in the context of continuing closer relationships between our churches (1989 Churchwide Assembly, ELCA, Reports and Records, vol. 3, p. 834).

In light of these understandings, our report will include the following elements:

—A review of official agreements and other materials available to inform our consideration of Lutheran-Reformed relations in the future;

—An analysis of problems encountered in the reception of previous dialogues in this country;

—A proposal for an applicable confessional hermeneutics;

—A discussion of specific theological topics as a test for the common ground necessary and sufficient for full church fellowship;

—The suggestion of a framework for the future agenda of an ongoing theological dialogue on questions which need to be addressed together in the fellowship of our churches;

—Appropriate recommendations for official action by our churches.

C. PARTICIPATING CHURCHES

The following churches were participants in the present Conversations. For benefit of the reader, we will give a list of their governing documents, church orders, and liturgical books in an appendix at the end of our document.

The Reformed Church in America (RCA)

Founded in 1628, this church grew out of the Reformed Church of the Netherlands.[4] It holds the Apostles', Nicene, and Athanasian Creeds and the Belgic Confession of Faith, the Heidelberg Catechism with its Compendium, and the Canons of the Synod of Dort as its doctrinal standards. While the RCA has never adopted a contemporary confession, a statement of faith entitled *Our Song of Hope* (1978) has been approved for use in the churches of the denomination. The polity of the RCA is presbyterian in form as prescribed in its *Book of Church Order*. The Church continues the four offices of John Calvin's order: minister of the word and sacrament, doctor of theology, elder, and deacon. Elders and ministers form the classis (corresponding to the presbytery in the Presbyterian tradition), which provides oversight and judicial process for the congregations and clergy located within its boundaries, while the General Synod acts as legislative and judicial body for the entire Church.

The RCA has a long history of ecumenical involvement. It holds membership in the National Council of Churches of Christ (NCCC), the World Council of Churches (WCC), the World Alliance of Reformed Churches (WARC), and is an observer at the Consultation on Church Union (COCU) in the United States.

The Presbyterian Church (USA) (PCUSA)

The Presbyterian Church (USA) was formed in June of 1983 as a reunion of a church that had been divided in the Civil War.[5] The two predecessor churches—the United Presbyterian Church in the USA and the Presbyterian Church in the United States—considered themselves heirs of the English-speaking Calvinist tradition which named itself Presbyterian after its form of government by elders ("presbyters") and used the Westminster Confession of 1647 as its doctrinal standard. In 1967, the United Presbyterian Church in the USA adopted a new statement of faith, the "Confession of 1967," and voted to place it in a newly formed Book of Confessions which contained the Apostles' and Nicene Creeds, several of the sixteenth century confessions of the Reformation, the Westminster Standards, and the Barmen Declaration of 1934. At the time of the reunion, the new church declared that "the confessional documents of the two preceding churches shall be the confessional documents of the reunited church." In addition, a committee was charged with drafting a brief statement of faith. As a result of this initiative "A Brief Confession of Faith" was adopted by the General Assembly in June 1991 and incorporated into the Book of Confessions.

The Presbyterian Church (USA) maintains wide ecumenical relationships on all of its four levels of governance. The General Assembly is a member of the WCC, the NCCC, WARC, and the Caribbean and North American Area of the Alliance, as well as the Consultation on Church Union. Its middle governing bodies, synods, and presbyteries throughout the country are active participants in local and regional councils and associations of churches, and local churches are almost uniformly involved in various levels of cooperation with neighboring parishes of other denominations and confessions. The *Book of Order* contains both a prefatory chapter on

14

"The Church and Its Unity" and a chapter specifically focused on relationships. The Constitution furthermore provides for transfer of ministers to and from churches with whom the PCUSA is "in correspondence" following the constitutional conditions for transfer of ministers among its own presbyteries.

The United Church of Christ (UCC)

The United Church of Christ, constituted in 1957, is an organic union merging confessional and covenantal traditions. Bringing together the North American Congregational Christian Churches and the Evangelical and Reformed Church of continental background, the UCC has Calvinist roots on both sides of its lineage and a Lutheran connection through its Evangelical Synod heritage.[6]

The *Basis of Union* that brought the Church into existence sets forth a "confession . . . embodying those things most surely believed and taught among us," seeking to be in continuity with "the ecumenical creeds" and the "evangelical confessions of the Reformation." In the Congregational tradition, the covenants and confessions include the Cambridge Platform/Westminster Confession and the Savoy Declaration of 1658;[7] in the Evangelical and Reformed tradition, the Heidelberg Catechism, the Augsburg Confession, and Luther's Small Catechism. The creeds that appear in the *Book of Worship* and the hymnals are the Apostles' Creed and the Nicene Creed. According to the Preamble to its Constitution, the United Church of Christ "claims as its own the faith of the historic Church expressed the ancient creeds and reclaimed in the basic insights of the Protestant Reformers." Further, "it affirms the responsibility of the Church in each generation to make this faith its own in reality of worship, in honesty of thought and expression, and in purity of heart before God."

The mixed congregational-presbyterial polity of the UCC means that, in council (as General Synod), it owns and makes doctrinal statements and liturgical standards which represent patterns of belief in its congregations and which guide its corporate life. These statements and standards, in turn, function as "testimony" to local congregations where the authority for "testing" membership is lodged.

The Church corporate ordains its pastors through regional judicatories which normally employ a rite from the UCC Book of Worship that includes the preamblic confession and the candidate's acceptance of "the faith and order of the United Church of Christ." Accreditation of ministers is by signature of the president of the Church and the judicatory representative with official listing in the UCC Yearbook, and local standing is in the Association.

The Evangelical Lutheran Church in America (ELCA)

On January 1, 1988, the Evangelical Lutheran Church in America came into existence. This church body is the youngest among the Lutheran churches in North America. At the same time, it is the oldest, tracing its history through its predecessors to the mid-1600s in the area now known as New York.[8] The church was created by the uniting of the Lutheran Church in America (LCA), the American Lutheran Church (ALC), and the Association of Evangelical Lutheran Churches (AELC), which in turn had been formed in the 1960s and 1970s through several mergers and one split of earlier Lutheran church bodies.[9] According to the "Confession of Faith" at the beginning of its Constitution, the ELCA recognizes the Unaltered Augsburg Confession as a "true witness to the Gospel" and accepts the other confessional writings in the Book of Concord as "further valid interpretations" of the church's faith. On that basis it is in communion with most Lutheran churches in the world through its membership in the Lutheran World Federation.

At its Churchwide Assembly in August 1991, the ELCA adopted an official policy statement entitled "Ecumenism: The Vision of the ELCA," which seeks to clarify its ecumenical stance. On the matter of Reformed-Lutheran relations, it states: "The commitments to fuller relationships with the Reformed Church in America and the Presbyterian Church (USA) made in 1986 by the three uniting churches were left as a challenge to the ELCA."[10]

D. REVIEW OF RESOURCES

The present Conversations are assisted by a wealth of existing materials on Lutheran-Reformed relations. They include historical and theological studies, operative agreements, proposed models of cooperation and fellowship, and recent official statements by other groups. Among the most important materials from overseas are the documents connected with the "Leuenberg Agreement," which established church fellowship between churches of the Reformation in Europe (1973). In the fall of 1988, a Consultation on the Leuenberg Agreement was held in Chicago, sponsored by the

Office for Ecumenical Affairs of the ELCA. Its proceedings, including the text of the Agreement, have been published in a volume entitled *The Leuenberg Agreement and Lutheran-Reformed Relationships* (Augsburg 1989).[11] The Consultation introduced the members of our Conversations to the central documents of the pre-Leuenberg dialogue in Europe: the Arnoldshain Theses on the Lord's Supper (1957) and its precursor documents; the Schauenburg texts of 1964-67 on such themes as "Word of God," "the Law," "Confession of Faith," "Boundaries of the Church," and similar materials from other contexts.[12] It also provided valuable information about the continuing dialogue among the signatory churches of Leuenberg and its published results on such issues as "The Doctrine of the Two Kingdoms and the Sovereignty of Jesus Christ," "Ministry, Ministries, Service, Ordination" (Sigtuna, 1976; Driebergen, 1981), "Baptismal Practice," and "Relationship to the Worldwide Ecumenical Movement" (Strasbourg, 1987).[13] The members of our Conversations also had access to a preliminary text presenting the five Unity Documents of the Communion of Churches in Indonesia (1984), which includes Lutheran and Reformed churches.[14] Finally, the Conversations took careful note of the most recent report of the Lutheran-Reformed Dialogue team on the international level, which was published in 1989 as "Report of the Joint Commission of the LWF and the WARC" under the title *Toward Church Fellowship.*[15]

E. THE RESULTS OF PREVIOUS WORK

The Leuenberg documents and those from Indonesia reflect formal agreements by which full church fellowship has already been declared and is now in the process of being "realized." The Joint Commission Report of 1989, *Toward Church Fellowship,* "encourages other churches to confirm for themselves the reality of this unity in Christ through such a declaration of full communion" (p. 28). Participants in the present Conversations are grateful for the immense help they received for their own work from these sources. Instructed by the labors of others, they are nevertheless aware of the limitations of these efforts in serving the specific situation in the United States. The Leuenberg Agreement grew out of, and speaks to, the specific experience of European Christians in the post-war era of the 20th century. The Indonesian documents belong in a situation where the agenda is one church in and for one nation. *Toward Church Fellowship* presents an impassioned plea for greater fellowship wherever Lutheran and Reformed Christians live together, but it does not relieve the churches of their responsibility to speak and act for themselves.

Our response to such an appeal and to the actions taken in other contexts must consider the specific character of Christianity in North America. In a society of free churches, the immigrant communities of the two traditions were very serious and intentional about their identity, one often defining itself in opposition to the other. Many Reformed and Lutheran Christians came to this country with the expectation of exercising their religious freedom by cultivating faithfully their particular heritage. In a number of cases this included some form of Lutheran-Reformed fellowship. In others, however, it eventuated in perhaps even stricter separation than was present elsewhere.

The American experience exposed each tradition to new opportunities as well as dangers. The evangelical revivalism of the frontier exercised a strong influence, especially on those immigrants who had been shaped by Pietism in Europe. Some leaders advocated adjusting confessional commitments to the "new methods" of the American scene. But each tradition also experienced confessional and liturgical revival in the nineteenth century, partly under the influence of a changing church scene in Europe, partly through the convictions of a new generation of self-consciously confessional theologians such as John W. Nevin and Charles Hodge on the Reformed side or Charles Porterfield Krauth and C. F. W. Walther on the Lutheran. These developments cast a long shadow, especially on the Lutheran side, as a warning against pan-Protestant homogenization.

Today, the experience of living together in an extremely mobile society makes it likely that "most people already believe that the historic Reformed-Lutheran disagreements no longer warrant division."[16] It is certainly true that most Lutheran and Reformed Christians no longer desire identity based on such fact as linguistic, ethnic, and cultural cohesion of immigrant groups. Yet, for reasons probably both theological and nontheological, faithfulness to a particular denominational heritage in the midst of the pluralism of American society is an equally strong fact of American life—if not of the majority of lay members in our churches, then certainly among the clergy. We value highly such loyalty to heritage and believe that our ecumenical commitment can only profit by its integrity and moral power.

The material before us as a result of the first three rounds of dialogue between Reformed and Lutheran churches in this country bears eloquent witness this peculiar situation. Despite its emphasis on basic theological consensus in most issues under discussion and a hopeful outlook toward the future, the Report of the first round of dialogue also sounded a note of caution. The difficulty of some Lutheran participants with the stated consensus is formulated in para. 10:

> Our churches are not in full agreement on the practice of inter-communion because they hold different views of the relation of doctrine to the unity of the Church (*Marburg Revisited*, p. 104),

even though a "Supplementary Statement" adopted by the group later seems to go farther:

> Intercommunion between churches . . . is not only permissible but demanded wherever there is agreement in the gospel. Such agreement means proclamation of the same gospel as the good news of God's reconciling work in Christ rather than uniformity in theological formulation (*Marburg Revisited*, p. 183, #5).

The official silence of the churches in regard to the recommendations of *Marburg Revisited* underscored the difficulty.

In their final report made public in 1974, the members of the second round of dialogue explained that their aim was "to test and deepen" the consensus expressed in *Marburg Revisited* "without ignoring remaining differences" (*An Invitation to Action*, p. 54). Faced with the challenge of the Leuenberg Agreement, which was about to be implemented by the European churches at that time, they rejected the option to recommend that Leuenberg also be sent to the churches in this country to be signed. Prominent among the reasons cited was "our peculiar and specific history in North America," but even more important was the criticism voiced by "some" that the Leuenberg Agreement contained "ambiguities and compromises" (p. 56). The "some" did not sit on the Reformed side. Reformed participants pointed out that "most of the Reformed churches have for a long time taught and practiced Communion open to all Christians and recognized the ordination of ministers of other churches" (p. 57). Some Lutherans, however, especially members of the Lutheran Church–Missouri Synod, interpreted their confessional heritage as excluding the "full pulpit and altar fellowship" called for by the Leuenberg Agreement without a more

complete demonstration of doctrinal unity. With considerable regret, the Dialogue concluded: "We attempted to express our unity
in terms other than Leuenberg but were unsuccessful" (p. 56).

The introduction to the joint statements of the third round of
Dialogue in *An Invitation to Action* echoed this regret but proceeded
at once to affirm "the strong affinities in doctrine and practice"
between the Lutheran and Reformed traditions. On the basis of
this affirmation, the Dialogue members called upon the participating churches to

a. Recognize one another as churches in which the gospel is
proclaimed and the sacraments administered according to the
ordinance of Christ.

b. Recognize as both valid and effective one another's ordained
ministries which announce the gospel of Christ and administer
the sacraments of faith as their chief responsibility.

c. Recognize one another's celebrations of the Lord's Supper as
a means of grace in which Christ grants communion with himself,
assures us of the forgiveness of sins, and pledges life eternal.

d. Enter into a process of reception of this report. . . (pp. 4-5)

While it developed its own "joint statements" on justification, the
Lord's Supper, and ministry, the Dialogue built explicitly "on the
earlier work of the theologians of our churches" and called attention
"to the full fellowship in sacraments and ministries already experienced in Europe for more than ten years under the Leuenberg
Agreement" (3.7, p. 4). But these appeals and the work of the group
itself still proved insufficient to overcome the deep-seated hesita-
tions, signaled in the earlier rounds, among a significant number
of Lutheran clergy and laity. The official response of one of the
predecessor bodies of the ELCA, the LCA, spoke on the one hand
of recognizing the PCUSA and the RCA "as churches in which the
gospel is preached and taught" and of "their ordained ministers
who announce the gospel of Christ and administer the sacraments
of faith as their chief responsibility," yet it did not recommend
establishing "full communion" with these churches, calling instead
for further elaboration of the conclusions reached in *An Invitation
to Action*. When the churches became serious about testing among
their members the assumed consensus, they made a number of
discoveries: despite the immense changes in American society
which have led to close relations between Lutheran and Reformed

congregations, fundamental theological differences from the sixteenth century are still relevant and keenly felt; controversial issues of differences in ethos and church order are still perceived in the order, organization, and daily life of the institutional churches; a new common language for the reconciliation of the old theological differences has not yet been found, despite the emergence of modern theologies moving freely across denominational lines; and a certain uneasiness about the theological basis for intercommunion and exchange of ministers, already widely practiced between Reformed and Lutheran congregations and their members, still persists. In addition, the two traditions have differing histories of ecumenical dialogue with other Christians since the 1960s, with the weight of eight series of Lutheran-Roman Catholic dialogue reports exercising a strong influence among Lutherans and fostering a tendency to raise Lutheran confessional and sacramental self-awareness. These developments must be taken seriously if progress toward the goal of full communion between our churches is to be achieved.

2

Confessional Commitment and Ecclesial Diversity

A. HISTORICAL CONSIDERATIONS

The issue of faithfulness to a particular confessional tradition, of course, has its roots in the tragic divisions in sixteenth-century Europe that shaped a new historical period, the "age of confessionalism" (Troeltsch). At the end of the century, it was not only political boundaries but also doctrine that defined the perimeters of one's church in a very real way. Required doctrinal subscription by the clergy to different sets of confessions was now a clear expression of the actual division of regional churches which, in the political climate of the ending century, had become a European reality. This did not mean, however, that there were sharply defined fronts between Protestant groups on all disputed issues. On the contrary, most reformers saw themselves as advocates of a middle position between two extremes, of which Rome was only one. What we today call "the" Reformed or "the" Lutheran stance was a mixture of widely divergent positions that were in constant evolution, still covering a great variety of doctrinal formulations—exclusive, inclusive, irenic, polemical—in an attempt to find the proper expression of the evangelical truth. With the deliberate drawing of confessional lines at the end of the century, "Reformed" and "Lutheran" churches tended to define themselves no longer as parts of the one church catholic but as the "true" church in contrast to false groupings. Over the following centuries Lutheran and Reformed Christians came to regard their identity as inextricably linked to the reaffirmation of the polemics of the sixteenth century. They often forgot that they had begun their journey together and had shared so much of the essentials in doctrine that union between Protestant churches seemed a realistic goal for most of the sixteenth century. The subscription to specific confessional norms required by the political authorities as a test of orthodoxy not only hardened the division of churches at the Lord's table and in congregational life, but led to deep-seated suspicion, intolerance, and at times outright persecution.

The Lutheran side had a relatively coherent history of confessional identity, beginning with the Formula of Concord (1577) which tried to unify the Lutheran witness after decades of bitter internecine strife. When the body of writings assembled in the *Book of Concord* (1580) became the standard of doctrine under Lutheran princes in their territories, the stage was set for the tradition of a strong-headed, self-conscious, polemical Lutheran confessionalism. In the nineteenth century, confessional theologians such as Wilhelm Löhe, August Vilmar, and Theodor Kliefoth in Germany raised their protest not only against the growing influence of rationalism in the church but also against "Unionism" with Reformed or other Christian churches and the neglect of the Lutheran Confessions. Many Lutheran groups emigrated to the United States from Northern Europe, fleeing from a forced union with the Reformed or from established churches where the confessional basis was eroding. One of their goals in establishing churches in the New World was the unhindered practice of strict adherence to the confessional norms of their tradition as a matter of conscience. Expressions of this stance have been a constant reminder that confessional subscription is taken with utmost seriousness in many Lutheran circles.

When the Arnoldshain Theses on the Lord's Supper were adopted by a Study Commission of the German Church (EKD) in 1957, one Lutheran member refused to sign because of confessional objections.[17] The same happened in 1988 when a Lutheran theologian registered her dissent from the international report *Toward Church Fellowship* (p. 84). In the most recent round of the Lutheran-Reformed Dialogue in the United States the participants from the

Lutheran Church-Missouri Synod filed a minority report which states:

> Since The Lutheran Church-Missouri Synod establishes altar and pulpit fellowship with other church bodies only after substantial agreement has been reached in all of the doctrines of Scripture, the LCMS participants cannot at this time concur . . . (*An Invitation to Action*, p. 8).

Confessional norms and confessional identity developed differently on the Reformed side. It must be remembered that, under the empire in the sixteenth century, Reformed churches and their princes were interested in minimizing differences with the Lutheran side since they were not covered independently under most edicts of toleration such as the Peace of Augsburg (1555). Their confessions did not have the same function of determining church membership through adherence to specific doctrines spelled out in terms of a negotiated consensus in an authoritative book of confessional texts. In fact, Reformed "confessions" were rarely consensus documents like the *Consensus Tigurinus* of 1549 or the First and Second Helvetic Confession (1536 and 1561).[18] Many of them were more in the genre of church orders, setting doctrinal standards as part of the regulations for church life and public worship in a specific place at a particular time. Examples are the early Swiss confessions of Zurich (1523), Bern (1528), Basel (1534), Lausanne (1536), Geneva, and later the French (1559), Belgic (1561), Scots (1560), and Hungarian (1562) Confessions. Some of these writings, especially the Heidelberg Catechism of 1563, enjoyed wide respect and use in combination with others. In the seventeenth century, the Canons of the Synod of Dort (1619) emerged as a rallying point of orthodox Reformed doctrine, just as the Westminster Confession and Catechisms (1647)became the doctrinal standard in the Presbyterian churches of the English-speaking world for the next few centuries and the Savoy Declaration (1658) among the Puritans.

Confessional identity, however, is not just a matter of formal norms and ancient or more recent texts that few members of our churches have ever read and studied. Nor is adherence to specific doctrines, expressed in catchwords or handy formulae, the sign of confessional identification. It is one of the peculiarities of a "confessional" tradition that it is not distinguished from others by specific doctrines but by a coherent approach to the whole of its theological basis. In each of our churches confessional self-definition arises from, and in turn shapes, a deeper ecclesial reality. Patterns of worship and mission, ways of piety and action, and histories of cultural encounter all contribute to this matrix of our respective identities. Formal statements of faith tend to verbalize the coherence and logic of these shared experiences and commitments of a community.

Acknowledgement of such subtler networks of meaning is a necessary part in the process of mutual affirmation and admonition. We have, therefore, spoken of the "confessions and traditions" that make us who we are. We believe that our churches will better understand one another and grow closer to one another as we open ourselves to the ethos as well as the doctrinal heritage of our partners in conversation.

B. CONFESSIONAL COMMITMENT

The Lutheran and Reformed churches engaged in the present Conversations share a common commitment to the authority of Scripture for the faith and life of their communities. They also acknowledge the importance of the ancient creeds and the Reformation confessions in providing the essential context within which the contemporary faith of the church is confessed. Each community explicitly states the nature of its confessional commitment in its official documents, and all require a confessional commitment of its ordinands. The language concerning this confessional commitment is diverse. Nonetheless, some common patterns can be discerned within our traditions regarding the authority of confessional writings.

Evangelical Lutheran Church in America (ELCA). The "Confession of Faith" at the beginning of the ELCA constitution states that the church

> accepts the canonical Scriptures of the Old and New Testaments as the inspired Word of God and the authoritative source and norm of its proclamation, faith, and life...the Apostles', Nicene, and Athanasian Creeds as true declarations of the faith of this church . . . [and] the Unaltered Augsburg Confession as a true witness to the Gospel (2.03-2.05).

Other confessional writings in the *Book of Concord* are accepted as "further valid interpretations of the faith of the Church" (2.06).

The ELCA language clearly suggests a prioritization of authoritative sources. After the mention of the Triune God, Christ, and the gospel, Scripture is given the status of "the authoritative source and norm," while the creeds and confessions are characterized as "true" or "valid" expressions of the church's faith. While the historic confessions of the church bear authority, that authority is derivative from the primary biblical norm. In addition, the canonical Scriptures receive their authorizing power from the gospel of Jesus Christ; "they record and announce God's revelation centering in Jesus Christ" (2.02.c).

The Lutheran rite of ordination requires ordinands to respond affirmatively to the following question:

> The church in which you are to be ordained confesses that the Holy Scriptures are the Word of God and are the norm of its faith and life. We accept, teach, and confess the Apostles', Nicene, and the Athanasian Creeds. We also acknowledge that the Lutheran Confessions are true witnesses and faithful expositions of the Holy Scriptures. Will you therefore preach and teach in accordance with the Holy Scriptures and these creeds and confessions?

Presbyterian Church (USA). The language of Chapter II, "The Church and Its Confessions," in the Presbyterian *Book of Order* (G-2.0300) identifies the place of the confessions in relation to the Scriptures and the ecumenical creeds:

> In its confessions, the Presbyterian Church (USA) gives witness to the faith of the church catholic. The confessions express the faith of the one, holy, catholic, and apostolic church in the recognition of canonical Scriptures and the formulation and adoption of the ecumenical creeds, notably the Nicene and Apostles' Creeds with their definitions of the mystery of the triune God and of the eternal Word of God in Jesus Christ.

The document articulates clearly the hierarchical relation that obtains between Scripture and confessions. Having affirmed the priority of the biblical norm, the Church identifies its confessional statements as "subordinate standards in the Church, subject to the authority of Jesus Christ, the Word of God, as the Scriptures bear witness to him" (G-2.0200). The "subordinate" status does not, the document makes clear, undermine their authoritative status in the church.

> They are not lightly drawn up or subscribed to, nor may they be ignored or dismissed. The church is prepared to counsel or

even to discipline one ordained who seriously rejects the faith expressed in the confessions.

The Church further identifies the "principles of understanding" enscribed in its confessions, namely, "the Protestant watchwords—grace alone, faith alone, Scripture alone." Further, the understanding of the primacy of the authority of Jesus Christ leads the Church to affirm the authoritative yet reformable nature of church confessions:

> The church, in obedience to Jesus Christ, is open to the reform of its standards of doctrine as well as of governance. The church affirms, 'Ecclesia reformata, semper reformanda' (G-2.0200).

For this reason the Presbyterian Church (along with other churches of the Reformed tradition) exhibits a willingness to formulate and compose new confessions as the contemporary situation raises new challenges to the church's faith. The most recent effort is "A Brief Statement of Faith," adopted by the church at the 202nd General Assembly in 1991 and incorporated into the *Book of Confessions.*

Ordinands in the Presbyterian Church are required to respond to two questions regarding confessional commitment.

> Do you sincerely receive and adopt the essential tenets of the Reformed faith as expressed in the confessions of our church as authentic and reliable expositions of what Scripture leads us to believe and do, and will you be instructed and led by those confessions as you lead the people of God?

> Will you be a minister of the Word and Sacrament in obedience to Jesus Christ, under the authority of Scripture, and continually guided by our confessions?

Reformed Church in America (RCA). The Reformed Church in America strongly states the primacy of Scripture in the life and faith of the church. "The Scriptures . . . are . . . the only rule of faith and practice; the concerted faith of the churches is to be tested by the Scriptures." The Church holds the Belgic Confession of Faith, the Heidelberg Catechism with its Compendium, and the Canons of the Synod of Dort as its doctrinal standards. In its Statement on Scripture (adopted by the General Synod in 1963) the RCA affirms that

> the Confessions of the Reformed Church are its response and distinctive witness to the truth of Scripture. They have authority

among us as faithful expressions of the Word, and have usefulness among us in so far as they are relevant witnesses thereto.
. . . Confessions are the work of men, having only a derivative
authority, and are always measured to their adequacy and finality
by Scripture itself.

Unlike other Reformed communities, the RCA has produced no
contemporary confessions of faith. *Our Song of Hope*, although never
adopted to be a confession, was endorsed by the General Synod
in 1978 as appropriate for use in the Church.

The RCA requires of its ordinands the following vow:

"I believe the Scriptures to be the Word of God and accept the
Standards [i.e., the ancient creeds and three confessional state-
ments] as faithful historical witnesses to the Word of God."

The United Church of Christ (UCC). The Preamble to its constitution
states the United Church of Christ "looks to the Word of God in
the Scriptures," reflecting thereby the Church's *Basis of Union*: "the
faith which unites us and to which we bear witness is that faith in
God which the Scriptures of the Old and New Testaments set forth."
As indicated in the Church's name, Scripture is read christologically,
for the United Church of Christ "acknowledges as its sole Head,
Jesus Christ, Son of God and Saviour." Accordingly, ordinands are
asked:

Do you with the church throughout the world, hear the word
of God in the scriptures of the Old and New Testaments, and
do you accept the word of God as the rule of faith and practice?"
(*Book of Worship*)

"The faith which unites" is further identified in the *Basis of Union*
as "that which the ancient Church expressed in its ecumenical
creeds, to which our own spiritual (forebears) gave utterance in
the evangelical confessions of the Reformation." The Preamble to
the Constitution states that the United Church of Christ "claims as
its own the faith of the historic Church expressed in the ancient
creeds and reclaimed in the basic insights of the Protestant reformers," and "affirms the responsibility in each generation to make
this faith its own in reality of worship, in honesty of thought and
expression, and in purity of heart before God." As mandated in
the *Basis of Union*, the General Synod of the United Church of Christ
formulated a Statement of Faith which sets forth in trinitarian and

doxological form a summary of classical Christian teaching. Supplementing the covenants of individual congregations or their inherited confessional lore, it functions widely as "testimony, not test" of the United Church of Christ's confessional commitment.

In the ordination rite of the Church as it appears in the *Book of Worship*, the preamblic confession is read, and the ordinand is required "to accept the faith and order of the United Church of Christ."

It is clear from the foregoing descriptions that the Lutheran and Reformed Churches represented in these Conversations bear common witness to the primacy of the gospel of Jesus Christ, the authoritative status of Scripture as the primary norm for the churches' faith and life, and the continuing validity of the ecumenical creeds and Reformation confessions as historical expressions of the churches' faith. All hold themselves accountable to authoritative norms in such a way that they identify the authority of creeds and confessions as derivative from the primary norm of Scripture. Since the Reformed traditions have neither agreed on a single common confession nor codified an authorized book of confessions, none of their historical statements of faith have equivalent status to documents gathered together in the Lutherans' *Book of Concord*. Since Lutherans have effectively elevated the ecumenical creeds and the confessions of the sixteenth century above later statements of faith, they have declined to add new documents to their confessional corpus. Thus they continue to assert the sufficiency of the historical creeds and confessions for the contemporary faith and life of the church. By contrast, the Reformed communities have shown a greater willingness to develop new confessions in response to contemporary problems and issues. By asserting the principle *reformata semper reformanda*, the Reformed churches seek to preserve a dynamic relation between the churches' confessions and the living Christ to whom those confessions witness. While Lutherans acknowledge the same relation of authority between Christ, the gospel, and the confessions of the church, they have drawn different conclusions from it.

These differences are not disagreements in principle; rather, they are complementary approaches to the complex question of the force and function of authoritative sources.[19] An authoritative text is meant to define and shape the "identity" of a community and its members and may indeed regulate their beliefs and behavior. But the text can serve such a function only insofar as the community "construes" the text in a particular manner, i.e., identifies some pattern(s) which will serve as the regulative or formative paradigms. There is a complex dialectic at work in the interaction between authoritative text and believing community. The text provides the authoritative shaping patterns, but the community must construe those patterns into an effective regulative whole.

Lutherans tend to emphasize the function of creeds and confessions as providing the regulative pattern for the church's common life; the Reformed traditions tend to emphasize the shaping role of the contemporary community of faith. Lutherans tend to focus on the sufficiency of the confessions of the sixteenth century; the Reformed traditions tend to focus on the need for the continual reformation of the church. Both traditions, however, acknowledge the primary authority of the triune God, revealed in the Scriptures and present in the living Christ active in the church. When Lutherans finalize and repristinate the theology of the sixteenth century, they need the corrective witness of the Reformed tradition concerning the continuing need for reformation and a fresh appropriation of the church's faith. When Reformed Christians overemphasize primacy of the contemporary situation, they need the corrective witness of the Lutheran focus on the authority of the ecumenical creeds and Reformation confessions. While there is considerable diversity within the Reformed communions concerning the force and function of the sixteenth-century confessions, we affirm the common commitment of all these traditions, Lutheran and Reformed, to the Reformation heritage that we share. We recognize our need of mutual edification and correction in the area of confessional hermeneutics.

C. Theological and Ecclesial Diversity

Since confessional commitment is essential for communal self-identification, it functions in part to define the limits of acceptable theological diversity within a community of faith. The question of these limits is particularly vexing within American Christianity today. Every American denomination, including those engaged in these Conversations, is struggling to achieve a balance between the encouragement of theological diversity and the maintenance of communal identity. Some bilateral dialogues proceed as if constitutional statements and confessional traditions accurately describe the theological and sociological reality in their churches. While those statements and traditions surely do identify important emphases in the lives of the churches, they do not fully account for the forces that are contributing to the current ferment within American Christianity.[20]

We are living in an era that witnesses a decline of membership in the mainline Protestant denominations. One of the key factors seems to be the phenomenon of "denominational switching" that frequently takes church members outside of the mainstream churches and has had two primary consequences: a significant decline in denominational loyalty and a significant increase in positive attitudes toward interdenominational activity. Increased levels of cooperation among Christian communities and the continuing mobility of the American population have combined to create a veritable "melting pot" within American Protestantism. Thus the theological and ecclesial diversity that might have been characteristic of some churches in the 1960s and 1970s has become commonplace within all of Protestantism in the 1980s and 1990s.

A second major change in the landscape of American religion has been created by the growth of groups organized to bring people with common interests and goals together. While their existence may serve as an indication of the vitality of religious commitment, they also provide an alternative locus for the development of religious identity among their members. To some observers it seems that the most important divisions within American religion today are not those that separate one denomination from another, but those that divide members within denominations along a conservative-liberal fissure. The civil rights movement, the protests against the Vietnam War, and the movement for women's rights have all contributed to the political tensions within American denominations.

We make reference to the current ferment within American Christianity for two reasons. First, the growing diversity within American Protestant denominations has affected all of the churches involved in these conversations. While a generation ago these churches may have differed dramatically in the degree of theological diversity within their ranks, today they share in the challenge of seeking a balance between historic identity and theological innovation. Second, the theological disputes spawned by the current ferment within both traditions could influence the perception of our Conversations in the churches and there have a significant impact on the reception of their results.

31

George Lindbeck has recently suggested that some Lutherans are pulled toward the primacy of the Lutheran-Roman Catholic Dialogue in part from a conviction that Lutherans should operate in continuity with the reformers at Augsburg in 1530.[21] They sought reform within the Catholic Church as Christians who stood in accord with authoritative Catholic sources. Some other Lutherans see the Reformation not only as corrective but also as constitutive event and therefore give priority to dialogues with other Protestants.

While many Lutherans would not see their ecumenical hopes accurately represented in either of these tendencies, Lindbeck has identified one significant "fault line" within the ELCA which may in certain quarters shape the response to this report. We appeal to Lutheran readers to consider our proposal on its own merits and not simply through the prism of current disputes in the ELCA.

In the final paragraph of this section we offer a model for ecumenical relations that has grown naturally out of our recognition of the importance of mutual edification and correction in the relations between Lutheran and Reformed churches. We do not equate this model with the "multilateral ecumenism" alluded to above; nor do we see ourselves taking a stand on the question of whether the Reformation was a corrective or constitutive event. Indeed, it is our hope that the model we offer might provide an alternative to the approaches advocated by polarized factions within our churches.

4. SATIS EST, THE UNITY OF THE CHURCH, AND THEOLOGICAL DIVERSITY

Since some Lutherans could not accept the proposal for "altar/ table and pulpit fellowship" from the third series of Lutheran-Reformed dialogue in this country, the current Conversations were initiated. Consequently the question has arisen whether the essential conditions for "full Communion" between the Lutheran and Reformed traditions have been met. In the language of the Lutheran confessions: Has the *satis est* clause of the Augsburg Confession been satisfied?

Our churches also teach that one holy church is to continue forever. The church is the assembly of saints [*congregatio sanctorum*] in which the Gospel is taught purely and the sacraments are administered rightly. For the true unity of the church it is enough to agree [*satis est consentire*] concerning the teaching of the Gospel and the administration of the sacraments. It is not necessary that human traditions or rites and ceremonies, instituted by men, should be alike everywhere. It is as Paul says, "One faith, one baptism, one God and Father of all," etc. (Eph. 4:5, 6)." (Augsburg Confession, art. 7, Tappert translation of Latin version, *The Book of Concord*, Fortress Press, 1959, p. 32.)

While the *satis est* clause was developed in a particular historical situation, it has become a more general principle guiding Lutheran participation in ecumenical affairs because it states the manner in which the doctrine of justification is to be applied to questions of the unity of the church.[22] The unity of the church is not a creation of human good works; rather, it is a gift of God's free grace made present to the church in the proclamation of the gospel and the administration of the sacraments and received through the faith that God's justifying grace elicits. Unity and justification (i.e., God's justifying grace and the faith that it elicits) are thus inseparable. Therefore only faith and the divinely instituted means of grace can be essential to the unity of the church in the gospel.

It is important to stress that the confessional stance of none of our participating churches demands further conditions for the realization of full communion. For Lutherans, the *satis est* of *Augustana* (CA 7) affirms that there is an essential core, a foundational understanding of gospel and sacraments, on which agreement, *consensus*, must be reached for the unity of the church to be discerned in several church bodies.[23] The German form of the article speaks of the "harmonious" (*einträchtig*) preaching of the gospel and administration of the sacraments. There is no insistence on full agreement in all matters. Rather the *satis est* denies any expansion of the necessary agreement beyond the core, i.e., the fundamental truths and institutions of the communion of saints called into existence by the gospel. This is the reason why the Confession of Faith in the constitution of the ELCA distinguishes among the norms governing the life and the relations of "this Church": the trinity, Christ, the living gospel, the Scriptures, and the historic creeds that are shared with the church catholic come first. Only then is the Unaltered Augsburg Confession mentioned as "a true witness to the Gospel" and the other writings in the *Book of Concord* as "further valid interpretations of the faith of the Church." The description of the later confessional writings as "further valid interpretations" does not diminish the respect for their value in guiding Lutheran thinking, but it does block any claim to requiring their language and thought forms as the exclusive expression of the fundamental truth of the gospel in the life of the church.

We have seen that, on the Reformed side, a similar priority of norms is operative. Reformed confessions and traditions have never implied that there was no agreement on the fundamental truths of the church's proclamation and sacramental life among Reformed and Lutheran Christians. On the contrary, Reformed churches and congregations have often been very open to living out the perceived communion with Lutherans in union arrangements of various kinds, locally, regional or in even wider contexts.[24] They practice open communion and allow an orderly interchange of ordained ministers with Lutheran congregations and churches. While they are conscious of sharing the basic Reformation teachings of "grace alone, faith alone, Scripture alone, Christ alone," they are jealous to guard freedom of theological diversity in the interpretation of the primary norms. No Lutheran who acknowledges the *satis est* of CA 7 can find fault with this position. Both sides can affirm each other in the perceived unity of the fundamental understanding of word and sacrament and admonish each other in the richness of interpretive diversity.

But how can churches discern their fundamental agreement, the fact that they could and should live in evangelical harmony *(einträchtiglich)* with each other? After a long history of distrust and separation, such discernment calls for serious theological and historical work that must assess their present theological self-understanding in the light of their historical disagreements with each other. It is to the task of this assessment at a number of crucial points that we now turn.

3

Doctrinal Test Cases

The mandate for our present conversations included the "discussion of such theological topics as Lord's Supper, christology, predestination, and mutual condemnations." In this part of our report, we will develop these topics as case studies to test the confessional hermeneutics developed in the preceding section. This will require attention to some technical theological terms which were crucial in the debates of previous eras. Such historical and theological work is important to undergird the integrity of our concluding recommendations. Our deliberations have suggested to us that we consider first the condemnations of the Reformation era, then turn to the Lord's Supper and christology together as parts of the one issue of "The Presence of Christ," and conclude with the discussion of predestination under the more precise topic of "God's Will to Save." In each case, we found it necessary to begin with a brief historical narrative before taking up the contemporary question of the implications for our churches today and their relationships.

A. THE CONDEMNATIONS

The concern regarding "mutual condemnations" reflects a general tendency in modern ecumenical relations to regard the removal of existing formal condemnations as one of the first steps necessary to move toward the goal of restoring church fellowship.[25] The background here is the practice of excommunication in the ancient and medieval church which, governed by set rules of law, effectively separated individuals or groups of people from a community of faith and from each other. Churches using the provisions of canon law, such as the Roman Catholic Church and the Eastern Orthodox Churches, must deal with existing condemnations in their ecumenical relations because these condemnations created a legal situation in which any form of communion was excluded on principle unless formal steps were taken to effect reconciliation.

The churches of the Reformation defined themselves outside of, and in protest against, the system of medieval canon law, which they denounced as a "human invention," and did not develop parallel structures until they entered the age of confessionalism. Thus, since condemnations for them were not an issue of canon law, at least during the early decades, the problem must be approached differently from the way the relations of all the churches of the Reformation to Roman Catholic Church require.

One can find a good measure of condemnation language in the writings of reformers such as Luther, Zwingli, and Calvin. In their passionate search for the proper understanding of the newly found truth of the gospel, they saw themselves forced to make distinctions, draw lines, attack, deny, reject, and repudiate other options. Their condemnations of "false doctrine" and of those who taught them (whether named or unnamed) were sincere but were aimed at reform within the one church catholic and cannot therefore be said to be "church-dividing" in their intention; that they in fact contributed to the division between the churches remains a historical judgment. While most of these condemnations uttered by the reformers themselves were directed against contemporary Roman Catholic teaching and practice, a number of them were part of an inner-Protestant polemic as well. Just as he condemned the Anabaptists, Luther regarded Zwingli as a danger for the entire cause of his reformation and did not hesitate to apply the biblical language of "heresy," "heretical," and "condemnation" to him and other "Sacramentarians." Zwingli and his followers, on the other hand, rejected this language in strong terms as wrong and unwarranted. While Zwingli and especially Calvin remained intent on reconciliation with the Lutheran side, they too felt the necessity of having to use the language of rejection, separation, and condemnation against opponents, dissidents in their own ranks, and anabaptist movements.

The use of condemnatory language, however, was slow in appearing in the official confessions of the Reformed and Lutheran branches of the evangelical movement. Attention must be drawn immediately to the fact that formal condemnations have rarely if ever been used in Reformed confessions against Lutherans or clearly identifiable Lutheran positions, even though Lutherans at times have claimed that they were. Any discussion of "mutual condemnations" between Lutheran and Reformed churches must take this phenomenon into account; the term may be a misnomer. Throughout the sixteenth century, Reformed Christians showed great concern for unity with the Lutheran churches, partly in order to benefit from the measure of religious freedom granted to "adherents to the Augsburg Confession" in the empire. There are clear statements of disagreement in documents like the Zurich Confession of 1545, the *Consensus Tigurinus* (1549), the Second Helvetic Confession (1565), the *Confessio Gallicana*, and others. The language of condemnation, however, is reserved for ancient Christian heresies, Anabaptists, and Roman Catholic teachings in the relatively few places where it appears. One is surprised to find that a thoroughly Reformed document like the Scots Confession of 1561 uses the term for those who hold an exclusively memorialist understanding of the Supper:

> . . . we utterly condemn the vanity of those who affirm the sacraments to be nothing else than naked and bare signs. No, we assuredly believe that by Baptism we are engrafted into Christ Jesus to be made partakers of righteousness, by which our sins are covered and remitted, and also that in the Supper rightly used, Christ Jesus is so joined with us that he becomes the very nourishment and food of our souls (XXI).

On the Lutheran side, the Augsburg Confession pronounces condemnations of a number of ancient heresies by name (CA 1-2, 8, 12, 18), of "the Anabaptists and others" (CA 5, 9, 12, 16, 17), and of a number of positions held by contemporary Roman Catholic theologians who are called "our opponents" (CA 2, 12, 16). Only one is aimed directly at an identifiable Reformed position, in this case Zwingli's (as well as Karlstadt's and Schwenckfeld's) supposed teaching on the Supper, without mention of names:

> It is taught among us that the true body and blood of Christ are really present in the Supper of our Lord under the form of bread and wine and are there distributed and received. The contrary doctrine is therefore rejected" (CA 10, German, *Book of Concord*, p. 34).

Apart from the substantive issue, which we will discuss later, the terms used here reveal utter seriousness in the rejection of false doctrine but also the uncertainty of the confessors about the exact scope of their language: the German text uses *verwerfen*, the Latin has *improbare* (not *damnare*). Luther's *Smalcald Articles* predictably contain the sharp language of repudiation including the terminology of condemnation (II.2; III.6; III.15), but even where the "Enthusiasts" and Müntzer are mentioned (III.8), it is directed at Rome, not at other opponents.

The situation changed with the hardening of confessional lines toward the end of the century. The Council of Trent pronounced condemnations in the strongest canonical form and, consistent with the legal consequence of excommunication, as a condemnation of persons: "Whoever says . . . *anathema sit.*" After Trent, it was the Formula of Concord (1577) which, for the first time on the Protestant side, employed the language of condemnation liberally and without restraint. Among its formal condemnations several were intended to exclude teachings characteristic of the Reformed churches in the area of the Lord's Supper, christology, and predestination.

We reject and condemn the following errors . . . (VII, Epitome).

We reject and condemn as contrary to the Word of God and our simple Christian Creed the following erroneous articles . . . (VIII, Epitome).

We reject and condemn with heart and mouth as false, erroneous, and deceiving all Sacramentarian opinions and doctrines which are inconsistent with, opposed to, or contrary to the doctrine set forth above, based as it is on the Word of God (VII, Solid Declaration).

The context, however, is important here. The Formula of Concord addressed internal issues debated within the Lutheran movement, not the external relations of Lutheran churches with others. The prefatory "Rule and Norm" discusses at length the question of "false doctrine" and how to deal with it. It argues that condemnation, not just mild rebuke, is necessary and appropriate in order to keep the Lutheran congregations in the "pure doctrine" and help them to "guard and protect themselves against the errors and corruptions that have invaded our midst." With this defensive purpose in mind, the signers do not condemn persons but doctrine. They attempt to define their own identity, to draw the line against others, to establish the limits, but there is no intention to end the discussion or "excommunicate" individuals, let alone entire churches.

It is clear from the foregoing narrative that the problem of "mutual condemnations" between Lutheran and Reformed churches in the sixteenth century is a peculiar one. Lacking the reference of a system of canon law, the language of "condemnation" remained sincere but imprecise. On the Reformed side, it was not used against Lutherans, and where it shows growth on the Lutheran side, its use was more the result rather than the cause of division between the churches. There can be no doubt that with the solidification of confessional identity under territorial law and with the hardening of lines of division in the seventeenth century, the condemnations took on ever greater significance in defining for Lutherans the image of the Reformed churches as enemies of the truth. They perpetuated clichés of strict opposition that served as justification for a separation in fact to which both sides had grown accustomed, without much regard for differentiation and development on either side. The condemnation in CA 10 may have excluded Zwingli but did not address the nuanced position of Calvin and of many early Calvinist confessions, as the Formula of Concord, art. VII, assumed.

We have reason to take seriously the rejections and condemnations of the Reformation era as an attempt to protect and clarify central truths of the one gospel recognized as normative by all Reformation churches. The decisions that crystallized in condemnatory pronouncements concern "weighty and important matters," biblical and theological truths which are as important for Christians today as they were then. They cannot be set aside as irrelevant. Above all, our respective confessional traditions witness to the gospel as the living Word of God in Jesus Christ and therefore call us to care for the veracity and vivacity of that Word among us. We have to ask with the same seriousness, however, whether, in the contemporary theological and ecclesial situation, their divisive role and function must be maintained. Under the same gospel there will still be different emphases, even different modes of thought, in which the whole of the gospel message will find its expression. Honest differences of interpretation, even of an interpretive framework, must be allowed. They must be confronted, but such confrontation may occur within the context of the same ecclesial communion. It does not require and justify separate churches. Even the condemnatory language among Protestants in the sixteenth century was rarely meant to rupture the existing community of congregations under the same gospel, but to call brothers and sisters away from perceived dangers by setting the limits of permissible speech within a particular community of faith and accepting the separation from persons or groups who held different opinions as a last resort only. When the perception of one's own position no longer excludes that of the other side, or when the other side has changed and does not recognize itself in that which has been condemned, the separation must be ended and the condemnations must be revoked. We believe that such is the situation today between our churches. Replacing the polemics and formal condemnations of earlier times, our model of mutual affirmation and admonition within a fellowship of churches recognizing their unity in the understanding of the gospel and of the gift of the sacraments provides a framework for continuing theological reflection without the need of perpetuating the existing divisions. Condemnations wherever they exist cease to exercise their divisive function when they are seen as important "no-trespassing" signs on a road being traveled together as part of a common life in ecclesial communion.

In dealing with "the doctrinal condemnations of the Reformation Era," the Leuenberg Agreement adopted a clear, syllogistic argumentation. It noted the theological agreement reached on each of the points at issue and concluded on this basis that the condemnations were no longer applicable to the doctrinal position of these churches today (39-41). We want to go one step further. Through their dialogue and conversations during the past decades our churches have become aware that the very language of "condemnation," "repudiation," and "rejection" is inappropriate for the confessional and ecclesial life of our congregations as they exist today. Too much has changed on both sides. We have become convinced that the task today is not to mark the point of separation and exclusion but to find a common language which will allow our partners to be heard in their honest concern for the truth of the gospel, to be taken seriously, and to be integrated into the identity of our own ecumenical community of faith.

B. THE PRESENCE OF CHRIST

In the polemics of the sixteenth century the debate about the presence of Christ focused on the understanding of the Lord's Supper and its christological and ecclesiological ramifications. To many Christians today these debates seem esoteric and purely

scholastic. There can be no doubt, however, that different understandings in this matter contributed greatly to the de facto division
of the churches. By the end of the sixteenth century, adherence to
specific formulations concerning the Supper seemed to be the clearest indicator of the dividing line between Lutheran and Reformed
confessions and churches. To be sure, during the early decades
there had been numerous attempts at reaching a unified evangelical
witness by negotiated reconciliation. At the Marburg Colloquy of
1529, Zwingli, together with his Swiss friends and the representatives of some southern German cities, were able to agree with
the Wittenberg reformers on fourteen central points of doctrine
including the Trinity, Christ's divine and human natures and his
work of salvation, original sin, faith, justification, the proclamation
of the Word, baptism, good works, confession, and the role of civil
government.[26] With regard to the Lord's Supper, they agreed

> that the sacrament of the altar is a sacrament of the true body
> and blood of Jesus Christ and that the spiritual partaking of the
> same body and blood is especially necessary for every Christian.
> Similarly, that the use of the sacrament like the Word has been
> given and ordained by God Almighty in order that weak con-
> sciences may thereby be excited to faith by the Holy Spirit.

The remaining difference is noted in these words:

> we have not reached agreement as to whether the true body and
> blood of Christ are in the bread and wine bodily. . . .

The Augsburg Confession in its original form, as well as in the
altered form of 1540 which Calvin signed, came close to serving as
a common declaration of the central tenets of Protestant faith in a
wide variety of countries and territories. The articles on the Lord's
Supper in the Wittenberg Concord of 1536 seemed to open the way
for a reconciled, united front between Wittenberg and the major
southern German cities, though the Swiss were not included in the
agreement.[27] Later negotiations, however, revealed a progressive
hardening of party lines. When Lutheran and Reformed theologians tried to reach a consensus on the eucharist at Maulbronn
(1564) and at Montbéliard (1586), their efforts were unsuccessful.
Political interests and personality conflicts certainly were factors in
the progressive alienation, but the different theological language
about the Lord's presence in the Supper became the clearest touch-
stone of orthodoxy in increasingly separated churches and confessional families.

On the Lutheran side this development was completed when the *Book of Concord* (1580) became the standard of doctrine in most Lutheran territories. At the same time, Reformed confessional and theological writings distanced themselves from language which they considered as unacceptable, which included much of the theological language on the Lutheran side. Clearly the article about the Lord's Supper remained central in the polemics. Divergent doctrine in this case led to different forms of the liturgical celebration of the Supper and different modes of eucharistic piety which mark the ethos of Lutheran and Reformed congregations to this day. Theologians still tend to underestimate the emotional importance of eucharistic practice for the experience of denominational diversity among church members. For many people, the "real" difference between a Lutheran and a Reformed church is the difference between a highly liturgical weekly eucharistic service with candles, vestments, crucifix, procession, sung prayers and responses, appointed lectionary readings, and the congregation kneeling at the altar rail to receive the elements, and a rare, very special, solemn, word-centered, deliberately simple, meditative and deeply moving community celebration, with the congregation communing in their pews and the elements being carried to each row from the Lord's table by elders or deacons. While this perception may be no more than a cliche which is contradicted by actual practice almost everywhere today, it does point to a strongly felt heterogeneity that frequently determines whether people are comfortable with a particular congregation or not, regardless of the theological issues behind the style of worship.

The historical reason for the great weight of theological differences in this area is fairly obvious. In the context of medieval sacramental piety, which was so important for Luther's own beginnings, the reformers of the sixteenth century assumed that differences in the doctrinal understanding of the eucharist revealed deeper disagreements: they expressed nothing less than different modes of doing theology and defining the perimeters of the true faith. Later interpreters, in order to define the heart of the difference, have pointed to antitheses such as Plato vs. Aristotle; *via antiqua* vs. *via moderna*; God's eternal rule vs. incarnation; heavenly vs. earthly reality; and the finite being capable of holding the infinite or not. In historical perspective, most of these pairs may look complementary to us rather than mutually exclusive. The dynamics of the formation of Protestant identities in the sixteenth century, however, highlighted only the irreconcilable nature of their consequences for eucharistic theology. People finally had to acknowledge the church-dividing character of the differences. Luther's reported word to Zwingli at Marburg: "You have another spirit from ours" and Zwingli's conclusion that Luther's insistence on the corporeal presence was of the devil demonstrate that in the name of perceived truth even the first generation was unable to cross the bridge to the truth of the other side.

On the other hand, the conviction that differences over the Lord's Supper might indeed divide Protestant churches grew only slowly. There was too much common ground shared by Reformed and Lutheran theologians throughout the formative period over against the Roman Church of their day. Against the Roman understanding of the sacrifice of the mass through the agency of the priest, of transubstantiation, and of the sacrament's efficacy *ex opere operato*, they all affirmed the theological canon of Christ alone, grace alone, faith alone, Scripture alone. They all concurred in the importance of Word *and Sacrament* in the church as the assembly of believers. They acknowledged the unique reality of the Lord's presence in the meal instituted by his own command and action. They agreed that in the Supper Christ is himself the gift to the believer, whose faith is awakened by the work of the Holy Spirit. They were all vitally interested in the assurance of salvation coming with the use and reception of the elements in the Supper and the implications for the sanctified lives of believers in the church as the body of Christ.

These shared convictions seem to cover all the essentials of a basic evangelical consensus that would allow Christians to live together under the same gospel in one and the same Protestant church. To sixteenth-century eyes, this was not necessarily the case. Even today, the understanding of confessional identity among pastors and lay people who are willing to consider theological factors is often determined by differences in eucharistic doctrine and practice. Centuries of polemics as well as forced church unions and conversions have perpetuated cliches and caricatures that nourish prejudice and the doubt whether the other side can be regarded as truly Christian and worthy of pulpit and altar fellowship. Whatever we may think of it, however, the reality of church life in the twentieth century has become increasingly oblivious to the sixteenth-century controversies between Reformed and Lutheran churches.

It is clear that the theological consideration of the old divisions over the Lord's Supper remains an ongoing task. Several decades ago it was furthered significantly by the common experience of

Lutheran and Reformed congregations together as a "Confessing Church" confronting the "German Christians" of Nazi Germany. In 1937, the "Confessing Churches" of the Old Prussian Union sponsored serious conversations that led to a proposal for a "consensus about the doctrine of the gospel." Articles XVII and XIX deal with the Lord's Supper.[28] After World War II, the newly constituted Evangelical Church in Germany (EKD) authorized similar conversations as the basis of probing the common ground concerning the doctrine of the Lord's Supper among Lutheran and Reformed member churches. The result were the "Arnoldshain Theses" of 1957, which tried to formulate in careful theological language a consensus leaving behind the exclusionary polemics of the sixteenth century.[29] The main criticism came from Lutheran circles, which saw their confessional subscription in conflict with the adopted language. The formulations of Arnoldshain as well as similar attempts in Holland and France were a strong influence in the drafting of the articles on the Lord's Supper for the Leuenberg Agreement.

Parallel efforts in the United States went in the same direction of reconsidering the old divisions and their accompanying polemics. The first round of the Lutheran-Reformed Dialogue in 1962-65 considered four comprehensive papers on the subject of the Lord's Supper and christology and adopted a "Summary Statement" noting basic theological agreement on most points. The third round, in its report, *An Invitation to Action,* laid out what the members perceived to be the existing consensus in a broad sense and stated: "We agree that there are no substantive matters concerning the Lord's Supper which should divide us." The statement was backed in the notes by a wide array of references to classical and contemporary eucharistic doctrine and practice in the participating churches.

It is important to note that, while the consensus language of these various declarations seems sufficient to many theologians on both sides to warrant full ecclesial communion, it has so far not been possible to reconcile fully the confessional formulations inherited from the late sixteenth century and their underlying differences in the mode of doing theology. These formulations have retained their integrity as honest and irreducible differences in interpreting reality and applying a theological perspective. *An Invitation to Action* stated: "Today we cherish a high regard for our ancestors in the faith who stalwartly proclaimed the gospel according to their respective convictions" (p. 16). The members of the present round of conversations are of the opinion that, if these different perspectives do not warrant the division of our churches, they must be seen as complementary, mutually enriching our common life and necessary for the church's total witness to the presence of God in the Lord's Supper. Each side has the responsibility to understand, uphold, and affirm the convictions and the fears of the other side while at the same time pointing to the deficiencies, dangers, and possible distortions to which each position may be subject without the witness of the other. It is in this spirit that we offer the following observations on the issues of Christ's presence in the Supper.

Lutheran emphases may be summarily described in this way:

1. Lutheran theologians traditionally insisted on the notion of the Lord's corporeal presence in the Supper through the Word. To them, only the bodily presence of the complete Christ, divine and human, seemed to satisfy the postulate of an incarnational soteriology. This did not exclude their interest in the role of the Holy Spirit and the faith of the recipients when they discussed the spiritual meaning of bodily eating and drinking in the sacrament. What they feared was the dissolution of the presence into a merely internal reality brought about by a subjective act of faith, and thus the reduction of the sacrament to a mere memorial.

2. Lutheran theologians stressed the link between the Lord's true body and blood and the elements, saying that the Lord is present, given, and received "in, with, and under" bread and wine. To them it seemed that only in this way the objectivity of God's saving presence here and now could be upheld. This did not exclude their talking about a figure of speech (*sunekdoche*, "a part standing for the whole") when bread and wine are called the body and blood of Christ. What they feared was that the physical reality of the Lord's presence, on which the certainty of faith in the sacrament rested according to the Lord's words of institution, was denied or weakened in favor of a spiritual symbolism.

3. Lutheran theologians asserted that even unbelievers or unworthy recipients eat and drink the true body and blood of Christ (*manducatio impiorum* or *indignorum*). To them only the acceptance of this consequence seemed to assure the reality of Christ's bodily presence that was proclaimed in the words of institution (1 Cor. 11:23-25; cf. 11:27). This did not exclude a strong emphasis on faith as the proper response to the word promising salvation and given in the tangible signs of bread and wine. What was feared was the

dissolution of Christ's objective presence into a subjective construction on the part of the believer or the community.

4. Lutheran theologians affirmed the ancient Christian teaching about the interchange of properties between the two natures of Christ *(communicatio idiomatum)*; what can be said of Christ's divine nature can be said of his human nature also. For them, only a complete exchange of predicable properties seemed to allow for the full incarnational paradox of the presence of the divine and human person of Christ in the Supper. This did not mean the endorsement of a monophysite christology which would deny the hypostatic union of two natures in the incarnate Word. What was feared was a Nestorian division of the one Christ into two, of whom only one, the divine person, is present in the Supper.

5. Lutheran theologians taught the ubiquity of Christ's human and divine natures after the resurrection and ascension. This was an auxiliary notion, based on the interchange of properties, which seemed necessary to explain the simultaneity of the Lord's bodily presence in many places at one and the same time. It did not mean the advocacy of a docetic christology that would slight the full humanity of Christ. What was feared was a local circumscription of the risen Lord that would curtail the divine omnipotence.

Reformed emphases, especially under the influence of Calvin, may be summarily described in this way:

1. Reformed theologians traditionally stressed the notion of the presence of the Lord in the Spirit as the mode of the presence of his body. Only this teaching, they held, allowed them to guard the ineffable mystery of communion with the living Christ in the Supper from profanation. This did not exclude their strong affirmation of the incarnational reality of Christ, the Word of God, truly giving himself to the faithful. What they feared was the perversion of a spiritual reality into carnal eating and drinking and the assumption of human control over the divine promise.

2. Reformed theologians insisted on the distinction between the Lord's body and blood and the elements: bread and wine are signs of the presence of Christ through which, while they remain distinct, the believer partakes of the flesh and blood of Jesus in the Spirit. For them, this view seemed to be the only way to avoid compromising the integrity of the incarnation of the Word of God in the man Jesus. This did not exclude their strong affirmation of a real presence beyond the naked and bare signs and the efficacy of the gift signified and sealed by bread and wine in the context of the

Supper. What they feared was a relapse into transsubstantiationism and crude sacramental magic.

3. Reformed theologians emphasized the Holy Spirit providing the bridge for faith between "sign" and "thing" in the Supper: for them, only the Spirit's activity in lifting up the hearts of the faithful people as suggested by the *sursum corda* ("Lift up your hearts!") and the *epiclesis* (invocation of the Spirit) of the ancient liturgies would ensure the proper understanding of the trinitarian fullness of the gift of the Supper. This did not exclude the teaching of a *manducatio impiorum* according to 1 Cor. 11:27. What was feared was an unwarranted reification of the gift in the community of faith and a loss of the trinitarian understanding of gift and giver.

4. Reformed theologians asserted the need for the distinction of Christ's human nature from his divine nature: for them, any confusion here would violate the once-for-all character of Christ's sacrifice on Calvary and obscure the true mystery of its efficient representation to the faith of the recipient in the Supper. This did not mean a lack of interest in the hypostatic union and certainly not a Nestorian separation of the divine and human Christ. What was feared was the soteriological consequence for the Supper of a belittling of the human Christ: the cross can only save when *our* nature is crucified; a deified human nature is no longer true human nature.

5. Reformed theologians taught the local circumscription of Christ's body in heaven. For them, this assertion seemed to be the clear implication of the ascension and was necessary to free the Supper from wrong sacramental magic to its true, intended spiritual use. This did not mean the denial of Christ's lordship over all the world here and now or the underestimation of his divinity. What was feared was that the philosophical construction of a ubiquity of Christ's human nature would jeopardize the reality of the historical incarnation and make the soteriological work of the Spirit redundant.

All of these formulations reflect the specific insights and concerns of many reformers during the sixteenth century, from Luther and the confessional theologians locked in battle over the Formula of Concord to Zwingli, Bullinger, Calvin, and the Palatine theologians of the Heidelberg Catechism. The differences do not detract from the broad consensus among them about Word and Sacrament as means of grace against the Roman insistence on unbloody sacrifice, priesthood, and transsubstantiation, a consensus of which both sides were fully aware. One could say that the dispute was not so much about the reality of God's presence in the Supper as about the "mode" of this presence and the proper way of expressing it in theological terms. At this point, language and emphases differ deeply, indicating nothing less than different ways of looking at reality and doing theology within alternative frameworks of reference. All the emphases, however, have a basis in the New Testament and in the theology and practice of the early church, at least in the view of the reformers. Both sides constantly referred to Scripture and history, finding their own convictions fully endorsed by these fundamental authorities.

Lutherans based themselves on the words of institution in the synoptic gospels and in Paul, and on Matt. 28:20, for their affirmation of Christ's bodily presence; the insistence on the *manducatio impiorum* represented their reading of 1 Cor. 11:26; they found the affirmation of the *communicatio idiomatum* and the ubiquity in the patristic tradition, especially in Athanasius and Cyril of Alexandria. Reformed theologians, on the other hand, argued for the spiritual presence from a different interpretation of the words of institution, from John 6:26-65; 1 Cor. 10:14-17; and the analogy of the Old Testament sacraments; their emphasis on the distinction of Christ's natures echoed the contribution of Antiochian christology and the Tome of Leo to the orthodox faith of the Council of Chalcedon (451). More recent biblical studies have explored the diversity of the New Testament testimonies in considerably more historical, literary, and sociological detail. Differing interpretations of these passages often cut across confessional lines.

For our present task this means that all of the divergent assertions and rejections among Lutheran and Reformed theologians of the classical age have a right to be heard and affirmed, but these interpretations are not uncritically received as definitive. Seen in the light of the beginnings, they are inclusive of each other, not exclusive, each of them necessary to express the fullness of the biblical witness and its patristic appropriation. At the same time, they warn each other and admonish both sides not to overlook the shortcomings and dangers in pressing for one side's concerns only. Thus, in all our theological reflection about the Lord's Supper in the churches of the Lutheran and Reformed tradition, it will be imperative to keep in mind not only the full range of the biblical witness and of the doctrinal tradition in the areas of christology, soteriology, ecclesiology, and the sacraments, but also the special concerns and emphases of the other side.

Lutheran Christians need to understand and uphold the Reformed emphasis on the Spirit, the trinitarian work of God, and the assembly of the faithful. Reformed Christians need to understand and uphold the Lutheran insistence on the incarnational paradox, the real Christ in bread and wine, and the objectivity of God's gift in Word and Sacrament. Both sides must heed the concerns of the partners, if not as a guide to their own formulations, then at least as no trespassing signs for the common forms of the churches' witness to the reality of God's action in the Supper. It should be clear to everyone that Lutheran Christians do not want to end up asserting a simple identity of the elements with the body and blood of the risen Lord, and that Reformed Christians do not want to be seen as celebrating the Supper merely as a memorial.

A common language for this witness which could do justice to all the insights, convictions, and concerns of our ancestors in the faith has not yet been found and may not be possible. But both sides can say many things together, enough to make clear to each other and to Christians of other traditions that the Reformation heritage of our churches in the matter of the Lord's Supper draws from the same roots and envisages the same goal: to call the people of God to the table at which Christ himself is present to give himself for us under the same word of forgiveness, empowerment, and promise. That this kind of a common language is possible may be seen in the attempts of various dialogue groups at attesting to the meaning of the gift of the Supper together. None of these affirmations will say all and everything that each side would like to say. But the witness to the common ground discovered in the experience of wrestling with the mystery of the Supper, in dialogue with each other, comes through loud and clear:

> The assurance of his presence is given in the self-witness of Christ in the instituting rite: This is my body, this is my blood. The realization of his presence in the sacrament is effected by the Holy Spirit through the word (*Marburg Revisited*, p. 104, #6).

> In the Lord's Supper the risen Christ imparts himself in his body and blood, given up for all, through his word of promise with bread and wine. He thereby grants us forgiveness of sins and sets us free for a new life of faith. He enables us to experience anew that we are members of his body. He strengthens us for service to all men (*Leuenberg Agreement*, II.2.15).

Both Lutheran and Reformed churches affirm that Christ himself is the host at this table. Both churches affirm that Christ himself is truly present and received in the Supper. Neither communion professes to explain how this is so (*An Invitation to Action*, p. 14, 2.1).

These formulations reflect the givens of the new ecumenical situation in the final decades of the 20th century. Biblical and historical studies have established new perimeters for the appreciation of each other's heritage and contribution. Ignorance of each other has given way to respect, and separation to life together. In looking at the differences in emphasis as they emerged in the sixteenth century, this could mean that Lutheran and Reformed theologians may come to appreciate afresh the efforts of some mediating figures such as Melanchthon, Brenz, Bucer, and even Calvin, who all worked fervently toward some formula of union. In terms of themes on which discussion must continue, both sides ought to agree that it is not the *mode*, but the *consequences* of the presence of Christ in the Supper that should be foremost on the common agenda: community, witness, proclamation, and the mission of the church in the world as fruit of the celebration at the Lord's Table enabled by the triune God.

C. GOD'S WILL TO SAVE

It may come as a surprise to many that, along with the issue of Christ's presence in the Supper, it was the difference over God's will to save or, in technical terms, the doctrine of predestination, that was perceived as one of the chief obstacles to Lutheran-Reformed church union from the later sixteenth century on. To any careful observer, it must seem obvious that both sides, from the beginning, shared in the fundamental commitment to centering their churches' teaching in the gospel of God's electing grace. Lutheran as well as Reformed theologians have consistently taught that our entire salvation depends on the grace of God and not upon human cooperation or ratification. There is an immensely liberating power in this insight: *God* has the first and the last word in everything that concerns salvation. God's freedom and sovereignty, but also God's eternal saving purpose, are the foundations upon which all comfort and all assurance of salvation rest. This conviction has deep roots in the witness of the Bible, where the theme of God's saving will is widely found, however different the answers to questions concerning its working might be.

Addressing this theme in the form of the doctrine of predestination, Lutheran as well as Reformed theologians claimed what they understood to be the Augustinian heritage in the church catholic. Against the Pelagian emphasis on the power of the human will, Augustine had stressed the devastating effect of original sin, the bondage of the will, and human dependence on divine rescue. He respected the mystery of God's electing choice but vigorously asserted the predestination of God's chosen ones to salvation as one of the chief articles celebrating the absolute priority of God's prevenient grace in everything. The Reformers echoed this doxological accent of the doctrine and deepened its christological foundation: Christ's cross and resurrection achieved the rescue. In him, "grace and truth" have found their dwelling place in the midst of a world of sin.

Both Luther and Calvin knew that the theme was bound to meet with human resistance. Luther said that predestination "tastes very bitter to the flesh," because in it "humanity is forced to recognize that its salvation consists in no way of its own actions, but that it can be found only outside of itself, namely in the election of God."[30] Calvin agreed that predestination causes profane persons "to carp, rail, bark, and scoff," but that because it is a "chief doctrine of the faith," it must be taught with boldness.[31]

Following Augustine, both Luther and Calvin took the "awesome doctrine" seriously as being thoroughly biblical. The Apostle Paul not only speaks of God's universal will to save in general terms (Romans 3; cf. 1 Tim. 2:6) but uses the term "predestine" *(proorizo)* in Rom. 8:28-29 in the context of wrestling with the "mystery" of Israel's election: "I have loved Jacob, but I have hated Esau" (Rom. 9:13). Neither Paul nor Augustine presumed to solve the mystery. Rather, they joined in the doxology of God's gracious will, which does include the salvation of those whom God foreknows: "Thanks be to God who has given us the victory through our Lord Jesus Christ" (cf. Eph. 1:11; Rom. 8:31). For Augustine, this teaching encouraged people to rely on God's grace alone, away from self-reliance and human achievement. It was a cornerstone of his argument against the Pelagians.

It is often pointed out that the younger Luther seems quite close to the strict predestinarianism more characteristic of certain strands of Reformed theology. His debate with Erasmus in the "Bondage of the Will" (1523) returns to the doctrine time and again as a bulwark against any Pelagian weakening of the fundamental truth that salvation is *sola gratia, sola fide,* and *per solum Christum.* For him, the soteriological context was primary, leading to strong statements both about election and rejection and echoing what he regarded as the true teaching of the church catholic through the ages.

The Augsburg Confession did not propose a special article on predestination. The doctrine as such was not an issue between Lutheran and "good" Roman theologians. Article 2 of the Augsburg Confession contains a condemnation of "the Pelagians," but the possible connection with predestination is not mentioned. Even the section in the Formula of Concord (1577) that contains the first confessional statement on the topic together with explicit rejections is prefaced by the note that "no public dissension has developed among the theologians of the Augsburg Confession concerning this article" (FC XI). The rejected errors concern the strict teaching of double predestination to salvation and damnation, which is said to endanger the universal scope of God's will to save and to take away the comfort given to Christians in the word and the use of the sacraments.

The Reformed side indeed had gone farther. Calvin shared Luther's soteriological emphasis fully. The early editions of his *Institutes* do not yet take up predestination as a separate topic; it was included after 1537. In the definitive edition of 1559, predestination's place in the system reinforced the soteriological accent (it is treated at the end of Book III on the appropriation of salvation) but added new weight to the logical consequence of God's election:

> We call predestination God's eternal decree, by which he determined with himself what he willed to become of each human person. For all are not created in equal condition; rather, eternal life is foreordained for some, eternal damnation for others. Therefore, as anyone has been created to one or the other of these ends, we speak of that person as predestined to life or to death (III.21.5).

It must be noted, however, that Calvin made very little use if any of this form of the doctrine in his exegetical, homiletical, and catechetical writings. It is also conspicuously absent from all major Reformed confessions of the sixteenth century, although most of them discuss election. This does not mean that nobody taught a stricter form, including double predestination. Theologians such as Theodore Beza and Jerome Zanchi developed Calvin's definition in the *Institutes* into doctrinal formulations which in various union negotiations during the 1560s and 1570s already led to bitter denunciations from the Lutheran side.[32]

It was only in the Reformed confessions of the seventeenth century that the article on predestination was spelled out in its strictest form, turning Calvin's formal teaching into a confessional standard of orthodoxy that included the language of "eternal decree," "reprobation" and predestination to damnation. Canon 6 of the Synod of Dort (1619) taught

> That some receive the gift of faith from God, and others do not receive it, proceeds from God's eternal decree. . . .

Even here, however, double predestination is not the point; Dort speaks of God passing by those not elect rather than destining them to damnation. The authors of the Westminster Confession (1647) took a harder line:

> By the decree of God, for the manifestation of his glory, some men and angels are predestinated unto everlasting life, and others foreordained to everlasting death.

> The rest of mankind God was pleased, according to the unsearchable counsel of his own will, whereby he extendeth or withholdeth mercy as he pleaseth, for the glory of his sovereign power over his creatures, to pass by, and to ordain them to dishonour and wrath for their sin, and to the praise of his glorious justice (III.3 and 7).

None of these confessions was directed against Lutherans. Dort fought the Arminian wing within the Dutch church, Westminster addressed the circumstances of the English situation. Yet, using the Formula of Concord as their norm, Lutherans typically have seen their own doctrine attacked in these texts. In the eighteenth century, J. L. von Mosheim cemented the confessional Lutheran attitude that in the canons of Dort the Lutheran doctrine was rejected.[33] Any leanings toward a stricter predestinarian doctrine in the footsteps of the younger Luther were further weakened by the Pietism of the eighteenth and nineteenth centuries, and even occasional controversies such as the criticism of the Joint Synod of Ohio by the Missouri Synod in 1881 did not lead beyond the position of the Formula of Concord, art. XI, both sides condemning the "contrary Calvinistic doctrine."[34]

On the Reformed side itself, however, the strict doctrine of a double predestination under an eternal decree has been consistently deemphasized in recent times. No confessional or official faith statement drawn up since World War I by any of the Reformed churches represented in our Conversations and beyond teaches it. Even references to a plain doctrine of election are hard to find. Presbyterian churches in the USA which retain the Westminster Confession as part of their *Book of Confessions* have officially disavowed the original text. A "Declaratory Statement" to this effect was added in 1903 and is held to be "the authoritative interpretation."[35] In the Dutch Reformed family, the case of the theologian Harry Boer, whose initiative to remove as unbiblical several sentences from the binding form of the Canons of Dort in the orthodox Christian Reformed Church (not a participant in the present Conversations) almost succeeded at the General Synod in 1980,[36] demonstrates that even in confessionally committed churches, Calvin's classical teaching has suffered a fate ranging from not being actively taught to being tacitly disavowed and even openly rejected by clergy and laity alike.

Under these circumstances it is hard to specify where the dividing line between our churches on the issue of predestination would run today. The Reformed churches never condemned the Lutheran teaching, even though they may have regarded it as incomplete and minimalistic. The Lutheran condemnations in the Formula of Concord, on the other hand, hardly apply to the contemporary expressions of Reformed confessional teaching in this matter. To put the situation sharply: rather than being divided over the doctrine, both sides seem to be united in an equally lukewarm endorsement and an equal embarrassment over any form of predestinarian teaching as part of their theological commitment.

If anything, it seems that both Lutheran and Reformed churches need to find new ways to affirm together the truth of a doctrine that is so deeply rooted in their common Reformation heritage but is in danger of getting lost in the churches' efforts to accommodate to the cultural mood of the time. There are obvious pastoral problems with a doctrine of predestination for a generation of Christians living in a culture that values human self-reliance and self-determination more highly than the analysis of the human situation before God which we find in the biblical witness and its proclamation through the reformers of the sixteenth century. God's unconditional will to save must be preached against all cultural optimism or pessimism.

Reformed Christians will engage in this task on the basis of an ethos that stresses the freedom and sovereignty of God: God's purposes will prevail, no matter how much we are puzzled by them or how often events seem to suggest otherwise. Nothing can separate us from God's sovereign love. Lutheran Christians will approach the challenge on the basis of an ethos that stresses the dynamics of promise, hearing, and believing: election is not a threatening, ominous doctrine, but a comforting message, a joyous expression of an experience of faith. It is an act of thanksgiving for the gift of faith so mysteriously given when it is given, a blessed assurance of sin blotted out and of undeserved acceptance. Neither side should have difficulty affirming and upholding the emphases of the other. All of these emphases are clearly expressed in their own theological tradition. There may also be room for mutual admonition. Reformed Christians may have to hear the warning against illicit speculation, a weak ecclesiology, the temptation to want to know more than what is revealed in Jesus Christ, and thus the danger of a triumphalistic, moralistic, judgmental distortion of the gospel message. Lutheran Christians may need to hear the warning against complacent self-assurance, pious passivity, and thus the danger of overlooking the importance of the responding life of faith among the elect lived in and for, not only against, the world.

A common language that transcends the polemics of the past and witnesses to the common predestination faith of Lutheran and Reformed churches has emerged already in theological writings and official or unofficial statements in our churches. Karl Barth's resolutely christocentric approach to the doctrine of predestination in vol. II/2 of his *Church Dogmatics* has done much to encourage the general replacement of "predestination" language by that of "election" in recent Reformed theology. Twentieth-century theology in general has questioned some of the harsher consequences of the sixteenth and seventeenth century formulations of the doctrine. There is here a fundamental agreement with the basic point the Formula of Concord was eager to make. The Leuenberg document expresses this consensus with commendable clarity:

(24) In the gospel we have the promise of God's unconditional acceptance of sinful man. Whoever puts his trust in the gospel can know that he is saved, and praise God for his election. For this reason we can speak of election only with respect to the call to salvation in Christ.

(25) Faith knows by experience that the message of salvation is not accepted by all; yet it respects the mystery of God's dealings with men. It bears witness to the seriousness of human decisions, and at the same time to the reality of God's universal purpose of salvation. The witness of the Scriptures to Christ forbids us to suppose that God has uttered an eternal decree for the final condemnation of specific individuals or of a particular people.

4

Setting an Agenda
for the Future Together

A. The Common Task

All previous rounds of dialogue between Lutheran and Reformed churches in the United States and internationally have recognized the legitimacy of theological diversity within and among our churches, yet they have also concluded that there is fundamental consensus or an underlying unity regarding the understanding of the gospel and the use of the sacraments in our churches, a consensus which all acknowledge is essential for church fellowship. The results of our own investigation of specific points of disagreement do not challenge or modify this conclusion. On the contrary, they undergird it further and again demonstrate its validity. We do not want to underestimate the theological significance of these doctrinal differences, but we are convinced that, rather than dividing the churches today, they should be accepted as expressions of a legitimate diversity that is demanded by the gospel itself as well as by the circumstances of the contemporary world in which the church's witness must be heard. The differences need to be discussed, but they can be addressed together. The task facing all Christian churches today calls for a vision of the great themes and priorities that need to be on the agenda of the ongoing dialogue. These themes cannot be dictated exclusively by our division and its justification in the past. They must arise out of the common concern that the gospel we share addresses all times, first and foremost our own.

The method of ecumenical dialogue has often been limited to a conditional logic, "if . . . then." If certain conditions are met, then certain conclusions can be drawn or certain steps taken. Instead we are proposing that a logic of "because . . . therefore" should govern the joint activities of our churches. Since we share a common understanding of the gospel, we must exercise our common calling in witness and service to the world. At a time when church and world experience the tensions that develop with increasing diversity, this new approach becomes especially important. As we engage in common confession and mission, we will also experience a critical reappropriation of our historic traditions, even as we serve an increasingly fragmented and divided world. To be responsible to the complex ecclesial relationships that have emerged between our communities of faith, the method of ecumenical dialogue must move to a more ministerial discipline, serving and strengthening our common convictions and Christian life, not our differences, important as they are. In that case, the logic of theological dialogue changes to "because . . . therefore." *Because* of this shared faith and mission, *therefore* it is incumbent upon our churches to present a common witness and service to a world that God loves and wants to save.

Our churches already cooperate in many ways in the task of making this common witness a reality in unified action at the local, regional, national, and international levels. Shared programs, facilities, and community services are a fact of life in many places, and jointly commissioned ministries in various forms are not uncommon. Theological dialogue has a critical service to render in the ongoing relationship between the Lutheran and Reformed traditions and has a word of witness for the mission and ministry of the entire church catholic. Such dialogue will serve neither the self-justification of a particular tradition, nor a partisan agenda in broader ecumenical arenas. Rather, it will affirm and demonstrate that Lutheran and Reformed heirs of the sixteenth-century Reformation together have a vital contribution to offer to a wider church struggling with the phenomenon of global diversity in the late 20th century.

Each recent dialogue between the Lutheran and Reformed churches of Europe, North America, and on the world level has concluded with a call for further discussions. *An Invitation to Action* suggested "referring any unresolved theological issues, such as the relationship between faith and ethics, and church and world, to a subsequent dialogue in the context of these new relationships" (4.d.10., p. 6). *Toward Church Fellowship* encouraged the churches "to engage in ongoing theological work and reflection together on the central doctrines of our faith, on the life of worship and liturgical traditions and on church structure" (IV.88). In a separate section, "The Continuing Theological Task," the Leuenberg Agreement states that the signatory churches "pledge themselves to their common doctrinal discussions" and draws up a list of specific topics:

> (39) The churches have the task of studying further these differences of doctrine which, while they do not have divisive force, still persist within and between the participating churches. These include: hermeneutical questions concerning the understanding of Scripture, confession of faith, and church; the relation between law and gospel; baptismal practice; ministry and ordination; the "two kingdom" doctrine, and the doctrine of the sovereignty of Christ; and church and society.

Structures for this ongoing dialogue were created. The work is being carried out by regional task forces, and several reports have been published and presented for further action.[37] On the basis of our Conversations, we would add for the future dialogue among our churches the topics of creation, the Trinity, the role of the doctrine of the Holy Spirit, ecclesiology, church, and world.

Whatever the framework, continuing theological dialogue is essential. It will require discipline and competence because the challenges that face the heirs of the Reformation are formidable. Some argue that the theological legacy of the Reformation is moribund because it cannot address the issues raised by modern secularism and cultural pluralism. A few have suggested that the witness of these traditions has served its usefulness and that, in the light of the reforms inaugurated in the Roman Catholic Church by the Second Vatican Council, exploration of the distinctive strength of this theological heritage will only serve to justify the perpetuation of a selfish denominationalism. But the testimony of our various dialogues makes common witness to our reconciliation in Christ, not to the dissolution or self-protection of our particular traditions. Taking up the unfinished business of the relations between Lutheran and Reformed churches in the United States after the creation of the ELCA, our Conversations have underscored once more the accountability of our churches to move ahead on the journey so promisingly begun during the years past, and to take up the broad challenges that face our common witness in the world. Among these challenges, we want to lift up three areas in which serious theological work holds out particular promise for equipping the public witness and service of our churches and through them the entire church catholic:

- Declaring God's justice and mercy
- Rebuilding theological authority
- Renewing the heritage for mission

B. Declaring God's Justice and Mercy

The gospel we share opens our ears to the cries of the hungry and homeless, our eyes to the plight of the poor and powerless, the disinherited and the war-weary. Through it we also hear creation groaning for the day when its rivers run free of our pollutants and its deserts bloom. Because Christ rose from the dead we have a word of hope to speak to those who despair of change and deeds of justice and mercy to do. In the partnership of our traditions, we can give a more powerful witness to the one who even now rules the world, enters into its pain, and shall make all things new. The language of justice and mercy, deeply embedded in the biblical portrait of the God of the old and new covenants, leads us to the very center of the most burning concerns of humanity. These concerns need to be addressed from an ethical conviction that draws on the strength of all our theologies.

Our dialogues have demonstrated that Lutheran and Reformed Christians often perceive a marked difference between their churches' traditions in the way they address ethical or moral issues. Some of these perceptions arise from caricatures or isolated examples. They are magnified by the "ruling myth" or image of what constitutes a "typical" Lutheran or Reformed stance. Nevertheless, any careful observer would admit some truth in the impression that there is a distinct, pervasive ethos in each of our confessional families that determines theological reactions as much as everyday decisions in a manner more clearly discernible by the other side than by a member of the same tradition.

Theologically, the difference is most evident in the ways the Lutheran and Reformed traditions testify to the reign of God over the world. Both read the same Scriptures. Both are confident of the ultimate triumph of the lordship of Jesus Christ. But they do not speak with one voice about how God's reign is exercised. The difference is often described as that between a Lutheran doctrine of the "two kingdoms" and a Reformed doctrine of the "kingship of Christ." Lutheran Christians follow Martin Luther in distinguishing two modes of rulership of the triune God: God's rule in Christ through the Holy Spirit in the realm of word, faith, and love; and God's rule through structures and orders in the realm of nature and society, under which all human beings live in responsibility for each other and for God's purpose in creation. Reformed Christians follow Luther and Calvin in emphasizing the one rule of the triune God over the world in creation, redemption, and salvation which, in Christ's death and resurrection, has broken the power of sin and evil in the world, opened a path of new hope for the world, and called the church to testify in word and deed to the present and future rulership of Christ as encouragement and warning for all in the midst of the ambiguities of human decisions.

The Driebergen Report (1981) on the continuing theological conversations mandated by the Leuenberg Agreement addressed this issue.[39] The participants came to the conclusion that the two doctrines are not each characteristic of only one of the two traditions. They do not exclude each other, though they have functioned in different ways as guides in questions of ethics. It is interesting to note that, beyond the confessional framework, both sides saw the need to discuss the role of "reason" challenged by and challenging faith as a major part of their endeavor. With this theme an important bridge to a wider dialogue with other religions opens up. Theologically, the Lutheran emphasis may invite the misuse of "abandoning secular action to its own laws and justifying existing social conditions as caused by God or simply accepting them as God-given.[40] The Reformed emphasis may invite an uncritical identification of the kingdom of God with a progressive transformation of the world and lead to moralism and legalism. Another suggestion was that the Lutheran mode of thinking

> sees the acting of the Christian in the realm of secular society primarily as the task of the individual. In this way it underscores the freedom of each Christian to decide and act for him- or herself.

The Reformed mode of thinking, on the other hand,

> begins with the assumption that the obedience of faith in state and society is a matter of the church as a whole also, and that the acting of each Christian must not be separated from this relation.[41]

This complementary and stimulating difference poses a huge challenge to the pastoral service and witness of the churches of the Reformation. Both evangelical clarity and obedience to the law of God are at stake. The ongoing debate about "justification and justice" is fundamentally an occasion for hearing the word of God and doing it. Our traditions need each other in order to discern God's gracious promises and obey God's commands. To reinvest this discussion with self-serving sectarian arguments would be no more profitable than the Samaritans and the Jews of Jesus' time disputing whether Mount Gerizim or Mount Zion was the place to worship (John 4:20-23).

C. Rebuilding Theological Authority

Our present round of Conversations was acutely aware that the way in which both of our traditions appeal to and use their authoritative sources has changed. This was particularly evident because of the participation of the United Church of Christ, with its less formal confessional identity. Although historical creeds and confessions have remained vitally important for large segments of this church, due especially to the influence of the Evangelical and Reformed heritage and its Mercersburg tradition, they are understood as "testimonies" rather than tests of the faith. They function as nonbinding but authoritative norms for the community, its theology and practice. It seems that today, more than in the past, this role of creeds and confessions has close parallels in the actual life of other Reformed as well as Lutheran churches. As we have pointed ed out, all the churches involved in this round of Conversations acknowledge a prioritization of authoritative sources in which the historic confessions are subordinate to the authority of Scripture and ecumenical creeds. On this basis, our section 2 above is an attempt to draw out the consequences of a contemporary confessional hermeneutics for the present situation. We all are conscious of the passage of the "age of orthodoxy," of nineteenth-century debates about authority and infallible sources, and even of neo-orthodox "biblical theology." The politics of modern democracies, equal opportunity, and globalization have altered the traditional authority structures within which our forebears ordered the world.

All of our traditions continue to affirm the Scriptures of the Old and New Testaments as the single most authoritative source for their faith and life. Nevertheless, the meaning of this principle is by no means understood in the same way everywhere. The impact of religious experience and rationalism on biblical interpretation, the rise of literary, sociological, and historical criticism, and the long-standing cooperation of biblical scholars across national and denominations lines have created a new environment for the application of the biblical norm. At the same time, a pervasive decline in biblical literacy among our people poses a growing challenge to the authority of the Scriptures in practice. Furthermore, the rise of a new scholarship exploring Jewish faith and communal life in the era of the New Testament presents specific challenges to these traditions in their theological understanding of the relationship between the New and Old Testaments. The increasing presence of Islam in the conversation about sacred writings will make an evangelical interpretation even more important, but certainly not easier.

Deep convictions persist in our churches, however, concerning the normative value and authority of the Bible and the evangelical witness of the Reformation. Our seminaries are remarkably strong in their scriptural studies, and our practice of worship and witness continues to be nourished by, and in constant dialogue with, the language and imagery of the Bible. While many educational programs in this country are interested in the biblical literature as religious texts of antiquity, Lutheran and Reformed exegetes are prominent in the ranks of scholars who interpret the Bible as conveying God's word of command and promise in and for the community of faith. Our traditions owe it to each other and to the whole Christian family to strengthen the theological usage of the Scriptures in the church of today.

The members of our Conversations group have become convinced more than ever that the probing of the biblical witness in common exegetical and hermeneutical work is one of the most important tasks of the common future. The Leuenberg Agreement sounded a similar note:

> (38) The common understanding of the gospel on which church fellowship is based must be further deepened, tested in the light of the witness of Holy Scripture, and continually made relevant in the contemporary scene.

It is disappointing to note that even in the thorough work of the Driebergen Report quoted above, the in-depth exegetical discussion is still missing. We would like to think that such endeavors would hold considerable promise for the deepening of serious relationships between the churches. Whatever the ambiguity of the human language of the Scriptures may allow us to conclude together, *sola scriptura* should at least mean "Scripture first."

D. RENEWING THE HERITAGE FOR MISSION

Much of the ecumenical progress of the past has been stimulated and sustained by the context of mission, the reaching out of the churches to the entire family of nations. When identified too closely with political imperialism, Christian missions were often guilty of exporting European and North American national, cultural, and ecclesiastical divisions. In their second and third generations, the "younger churches" of Asia, Africa, and Latin America have become impatient with this state of affairs and are no longer inclined to perpetuate denominational distinctions which contribute little to their specific witness and service. Today they come into their own as the instructors of the "older churches" of North America and Europe by increasing the awareness of the limited value of an imposed, enculturated Christianity. The insights of the global church are now coming home to the mission settings of our urban neighborhoods and rural communities.

The task of a new mission is also coming home in ways that pose a particular challenge to these churches of the Reformation. Dramatic changes such as the new role of women in society, new family systems, geographic mobility, and greatly accelerated schedules alter the traditional ways of religious instruction in family and community, prayer, and worship by which the faith has been transmitted in Christian catechesis. The rich intellectual and cultural heritage of our churches must be enabled to address and interpret the rapidly changing worlds of scientific thought, technology, and global communication. Problems of staggering dimensions, such as the growing disparity between wealthy and poor nations, conflicts among people of different religions, and the growing peril to the earth itself call for the clear witness of those whose very confession centers in the proclamation of God's law and gospel, God's justice and mercy made perfect in Christ Jesus. The question here is: Will the evangelical confession and tradition of our churches be used merely to defend old forms of Christian life and loyalty, or will the historic tradition of their witness in its diversity become a resource for a renewed mission through a worldwide communion of our churches?

This challenge will test the spirit of our churches, and those who serve them with a ministry of theological reflection have a vital contribution to make. The depth and intensity of ecumenical dialogue will not be diminished but will be directed by such accountability even more urgently to the task of a worldwide mission to which our Lord calls the church. In this situation, the logic of "because . . . therefore" will be even more demanding of theological sensitivity and excellence. "Because" of the fundamental evangelical unity of these heirs of the Reformation, "therefore" ever greater clarity and effectiveness will be required of the existing Lutheran and Reformed churches in their common mission, undergirded by mutual affirmation and admonition, in the context of the present world.

5

Conclusions and Recommendations

We have explored both our similarities and differences in an effort to discover whether our churches "agree concerning the teaching of the Gospel and the administration of the sacraments," i.e., whether our agreement is sufficient for the establishment of "full communion" between the churches of the Lutheran and Reformed traditions.[42] By full communion we understand a God-given unity, established in hope, received in faith, and nurtured in love. Full communion is both a faithful declaration concerning the current state of consensus among these churches and a hope-filled commitment to the visible and structural realization of that consensus in our common life. In light of the specific mandate given this committee, and on the basis of our theological discussions, we can name no "church-dividing differences" that should preclude the declaration of full fellowship between these churches. While the disagreements between our communities that led to the sixteenth-century condemnations regarding eucharist, christology, and predestination continue to shape and reflect our identities, they cannot claim to be church-dividing today and should not stand in the way of achieving "full communion" among us. In addition, we affirm that the differences among these churches of the Reformation on questions of confessional commitment, ministry, and ecclesial polity fall within the bounds of allowable evangelical diversity and are therefore not church-dividing. The course of our conversations has encouraged us to recognize in our results the strong logic of "because . . . therefore." Confident that our churches share a fundamental agreement in the gospel, we affirm that the basic conditions for full communion have been met, and we urge our churches to engage in common actions designed to realize this full communion in the lived experience of our communities, including the declaration of what has sometimes been called in our dialogue "altar/table and pulpit fellowship."

In discovering our agreement on the essential matters of the gospel, we have also recognized the important theological differences that remain between our churches in such questions as the understanding of the Lord's Supper and christology. These theological differences are, we believe, crucial for the ongoing ecumenical relations between these traditions. We view them not as disagreements that need to be overcome but as diverse witnesses to the one gospel that we confess in common. Rather than being church-dividing, the varying theological emphases among, and even within, these communities provide complementary expressions of the church's faith in the triune God. Throughout this document we employ the principle of "mutual affirmation and admonition" to make the different theological emphases of these traditions fruitful for each other and for their common witness in the wider church. The theological diversity within our common confession provides both the complementarity needed for a full and adequate witness to the gospel (mutual affirmation) and the corrective reminder that every theological approach is a partial and incomplete witness to the gospel (mutual admonition).

This present round of Conversations was charged with "exploring what next steps need to be taken on the road to fuller fellowship." All of our churches agree that this task is one of completion, not of revision. Much has been achieved already. All the Reformed churches represented in these Conversations have acted to accept the recommendations of the third round of Dialogue contained in *An Invitation to Action*, two of them before, one after the creation of the ELCA. With this decision, they have affirmed on their part their readiness for the mutual declaration of full communion with their new Lutheran partner church, the ELCA. We believe the time has come for all our churches to take this step together.

Our years of study of previous dialogues and the mandated exploration of issues and relationships have led us to the following unanimous recommendation:

That the Evangelical Lutheran Church in America, the Presbyterian Church (USA), the Reformed Church in America (RCA), and the United Church of Christ declare that they are in full communion with one another. In the specific terms of full communion as they are developed in our study, this recommendation also requires

(1) that they recognize each other as churches in which the gospel is rightly preached and the sacraments rightly administered according to the word of God;

(2) that they withdraw any historic condemnation by one side or the other as inappropriate for the life and faith of our churches today;

(3) that they continue to recognize each other's baptism and authorize and encourage the sharing of the Lord's Supper among their members;

(4) that they recognize each others' various ministries and make provision for the orderly exchange of ordained ministers of word and sacrament;

(5) that they establish appropriate channels of consultation and decision-making within the existing structures of the churches;[43]

(6) that they commit themselves to an ongoing process of theological dialogue in order to clarify further the common understanding of the faith[43] and foster its common expression in evangelism, witness, and service;

(7) that they pledge themselves to living together under the gospel in such a way that the principle of mutual affirmation and admonition becomes the basis of a trusting relationship in which respect and love for the other will have a chance to grow.

The principle of "mutual affirmation and admonition" which has guided our deliberations throughout this document offers, it seems to us, an important model for theological reflection on ecumenical relations everywhere; it also provides a basis for assessing the results of these particular Conversations for the life of our own churches. We rejoice that we have found a level of consensus that enables a declaration of full communion while respecting the theological differences among us, and we urge the commencement of a dynamic process of reception designed to lead to the realization of full communion in the lived experience of the churches of the Reformation.

Appendix

GOVERNING DOCUMENTS, CHURCH ORDERS, AND LITURGICAL BOOKS OF THE PARTICIPATING CHURCHES

Evangelical Lutheran Church in America (ELCA)

Constitution and Bylaws of the ELCA, ELCA, Office of the Secretary.

The Book of Concord: The Confessions of the Evangelical Lutheran Church. Theodore G. Tappert, tr. and ed. Philadelphia: Fortress Press, 1959.

Lutheran Book of Worship. Minneapolis: Augsburg Publishing House; Philadelphia: Board of Publication, Lutheran Church in America, 1978.

Occasional Services: Companion to the Lutheran Book of Worship. Minneapolis: Augsburg Publishing House; Philadelphia: Fortress Press, 1982.

Ecumenism: The Vision of the ELCA. ELCA, Office of the Secretary, 1991.

Contact address for publications: Office of the Secretary, ELCA, 8765 West Higgins Road, Chicago, IL 60631.

Presbyterian Church (USA) (PCUSA)

The Constitution of the Presbyterian Church (USA). Part I: Book of Confessions. Office of the General Assembly of the PC (USA), 1992 edition.

The Constitution of the Presbyterian Church (USA). Part II: Book of Order: Form of Government, Directory for Worship, Rules of Discipline, Office of the General Assembly of the PC (USA), annual edition.

Contact address for publications: Office of the General Assembly of the PC (USA), 100 Witherspoon Street, Louisville, KY 40202-1396.

The Presbyterian Hymnal: Hymns, Psalms and Spiritual Songs, Louisville: Westminster/John Knox Press, 1990.

Book of Common Worship, Louisville: Westminster/John Knox Press, to be published in 1993.

Contact address for above publications: Westminster/John Knox Press, 100 Witherspoon Street, Louisville, KY 40202-1396.

Reformed Church in America (RCA)

Constitution and Bylaws. Published by the General Synod of the RCA.

The Book of Church Order. New York: Reformed Church Press, 1982.

Standards of the Reformed Church in America.

Our Song of Hope: A Provisional Confession of Faith of the Reformed Church in America. With Commentary and Appendices by Eugene P. Heideman. Grand Rapids: Eerdmans, 1975.

Worship the Lord. James R. Esther; Donald J. Bruggink, eds. Grand Rapids: Eerdmans, 1987.

Contact address for publications: RCA Distribution Center, TRA-VARCA, Grandville, MI 49418.

United Church of Christ (UCC)

Constitution and Bylaws of the United Church of Christ. Published by the Executive Council for the UCC; 1991 edition.

Basis of Union, in: Louis H. Gunnemann. *The Shaping of the United Church of Christ.* (New York: United Church Press, 1977, pp. 207-225.

United Church of Christ: Manual on Ministry. New York: Office for Church Life and Leadership, UCC, 1986.

Book of Worship: United Church of Christ. New York: Office for Church Life and Leadership, UCC, 1986.

The Hymnal of the United Church of Christ. Philadelphia: United Church Press, 1974.

Contact address for publications: Office of the President, UCC, 700 Prospect Avenue West, Cleveland, OH 44115.

Notes

1. *Marburg Revisited: A Reexamination of Lutheran and Reformed Traditions*, Paul C. Empie and James I. McCord, eds. (Minneapolis: Augsburg Publishing House, 1966).
2. *An Invitation to Action: A Study of Ministry. Sacraments, and Recognition*, James E. Andrews and Joseph A. Burgess, eds. (The Lutheran-Reformed Dialogue, Series III, 1981-1983; Philadelphia: Fortress Press, 1984).
3. The papers of this meeting were published in *New Conversations* (New York: United Church Board for Homeland Ministries), vol. 10:2 (Winter/Spring, 1988), under the title, "Lutheran/Reformed Church Dialogue and the UCC."
4. For a short history, see Arie Brouwer, *Reformed Church Roots: Thirty-Five Formative Events* (New York: Reformed Church Press, 1977).
5. For a brief narrative account see Lefferts A. Loetscher, *A Brief History of the Presbyterians*, 4th ed., with a new chapter by George Laird Hunt (Philadelphia: Westminster, 1983).
6. For a fuller description, see the special note at the end. A historical narrative is available in Louis H. Gunnemann, *The Shaping of the UCC: An Essay in the History of American Christianity* (New York: United Church Press, 1977).
7. See *The Creeds and Platforms of Congregationalism*, Williston Walker, ed., introduction by Douglas Horton (Boston: Pilgrim Press, 1960).

8. See Todd Nichol, *All These Lutherans: Three Paths Toward a New Lutheran Church* (Minneapolis: Augsburg, 1986), and the entry "United States of America," in: E. Theodore Bachmann and Mercia Brenne Bachmann, *Lutheran Churches in the World: A Handbook* (Minneapolis: Augsburg, 1989), pp. 566-610.

9. The AELC had 110,000 members and was constituted by congregations that broke away from the Lutheran Church-Missouri Synod (LCMS) in 1976. A church of 2.6 million members, the LCMS is not in full communion with any other Lutheran church in the USA.

10. *A Commentary on "Ecumenism: The Vision of the ELCA,"* William G. Rusch, ed. (Minneapolis: Augsburg, 1990), p. 52.

11. *The Leuenberg Agreement and Lutheran-Reformed Relationships: Evaluations by North American and European Theologians*, William G. Rusch and Daniel F. Martensen, eds. (Minneapolis: Augsburg, 1989).

12. See the texts in Elisabeth Schieffer, *Von Schauenburg nach Leuenberg: Entstehung und Bedeutung der Konkordie reformatorischer Kirchen in Europa* (Konfessionskundliche und kontroverstheologische Studien, 48) (Paderborn: Verlag der Bonifatius-Druckerei, 1983); *Auf dem Weg: Lutherisch-reformierte Kirchengemeinschaft: Berichte und Texte*, zusammengestellt und herausgegeben vom Sekretariat für Glauben und Kirchenverfassung [WCC, Faith and Order] (Polis, 33. Evangelische Zeitbuchreihe, ed. by Max Geiger, Heinrich Ott, Lukas Vischer; Zürich: EVZ Verlag, 1967); *Auf dem Weg II: Gemeinschaft der reformatorischen Kirchen: Berichte und Dokumente des lutherisch-reformierten Gesprächs in Europa mit Beiträgen von Hans Georg Geyer und Marc Lienhard*, herausgegeben vom Sekretariat für Glauben und Kirchenverfassung [WCC, Faith and Order] (Polis, 41; Zürich: Evangelischer Verlag, 1971).

13. [Sigtuna Report] *Zeugnis und Dienst reformatorischer Kirchen im Europa der Gegenwart*; Marc Lienhard, ed. (Ökumenische Perspektiven, 8; Frankfurt a.M.: Verlag Otto Lembeck and Verlag Josef Knecht, 1982); [Driebergen Report] *Konkordie und Kirchengemeinschaft reformatorischer Kirchen im Europa der Gegenwart: Texte der Konferenz von Driebergen*; Andre Birmele, ed. (Ökumenische Perspektiven, 10; Frankfurt a.M.: Verlag Otto Lembeck and Verlag Josef Knecht, 1982); [Strasbourg Report] *Konkordie und Ökumene: Die Leuenberger Kirchengemeinschaft in der gegenwärtigen ökumenischen Situation: Texte der Konferenz von*

Strassburg; Andre Birmelé, ed. (Frankfurt a.M.: Verlag Otto Lembeck, 1988).

14. *Entering the Future Together: Five Unity Documents of the Churches in Indonesia,* Edward Nyhus, tr. (draft, n.d., typescript).
15. *Toward Church Fellowship: Report of the Joint Commission of the Lutheran World Federation and the World Alliance of Reformed Churches* (Geneva: LWF and WARC, 1989).
16. George Lindbeck, "The Reformation Heritage and Christian Unity," *Lutheran Quarterly* 2:4 (Winter 1988) 477-502; 480.
17. See Ulrich Kühn, "Abendmahl IV," *Theologische Realenzyklopäde,* vol. 1 (1977) 153-157; 155.
18. For the texts in English, see Arthur C. Cochrane, *Reformed Confessions of the Sixteenth Century* (Philadelphia: Westminster Press, 1966); Thomas F. Torrance, *The School of Faith: The Catechisms of the Reformed Church* (London, J. Clarke, 1959). A comprehensive collection in the original languages may be found in *Die Bekenntnisschriften der Reformierten Kirche,* E.F. Karl Muller, ed. (Leipzig: A. Deichert'sche Verlagsbuchhandlung, 1903).
19. For the following argument, see David H. Kelsey, *The Uses of Scripture in Recent Theology* (Philadelphia: Fortress Press, 1975).
20. For the following analysis, cf. Robert J. Wuthnow, *The Restructuring of American Religion: Society and Faith Since World War II* (Princeton: Princeton University Press, 1988).
21. *Dialogue* (Spring 1991).
22. See "Appendix 1: The Relation Between *Satis Est* and Full Communion: An Opinion from the Institute for Ecumenical Research, Strasbourg," in: *A Commentary on "Ecumenism: The Vision of the ELCA"* (above, note 10), pp. 105-118.
23. The concept of "fundamental consensus" is emerging as an important topic in ecumenical discussion; see the issue *Fundamental Differences, Fundamental Consensus* in: *Midstream: An Ecumenical Journal,* vol. 25:3 (July 1986), with contributions by Harding Meyer and others. It should be mentioned that the term has little use in Reformed circles.
24. Nineteenth-century Germany saw the formation not only of the Prussian Union Church under order of the king (1817) but also of "consensus unions," e.g., in Baden (1821), Nassau, and the Palatinate. On "union churches" in Pennsylvania, see Horace S. Sills, "The Union Church: A Case of Lutheran and Reformed Cooperation," in: *Hidden Histories in the United Church of Christ*, vol 2; Barbara Brown Zikmund, ed. (New York: United Church Press, 1987), pp. 13-31. *Documents of Lutheran Unity*

Richard C. Wolf, ed. (Philadelphia: Fortress Press, 1966), pp. 4, 45, 78, 80-85. A statement by pastors serving in union churches, entitled "Recognition of Ministry in Union Churches," was shared with members of this Conversations group in 1990 by Pastor Glenn L. Simmons, Assistant to the Bishop, Northeastern Pennsylvania Synod of the ELCA.

25. See Leuenberg Agreement, 17; cf. Marc Lienhard, in: *The Leuenberg Agreement and Lutheran-Reformed Relations* (above, note 11), pp. 28-29, and the discussion engendered by a Roman Catholic-Lutheran report, *The Condemnations of the Reformation Era: Do They Still Divide?*, Karl Lehmann and Wolfhart Pannenberg, eds.; Margaret Kohl, tr. (Minneapolis: Fortress, 1990). For our section, we found especially useful the study by Marc Lienhard, "Die Verwerfung der Irrlehre und das Verhältnis zwischen lutherischen und reformierten Kirchen: Eine Untersuchung zu den Kondemnationen der Bekenntnisse das 16 Jahrhunderts," in: *Auf dem Weg II* (above, note 12), pp. 69-152.

26. *Luther's Works*, vol. 38: *Word and Sacrament IV*, M. Lehmann, ed. (Philadelphia: Fortress Press, 1971), pp. 85-89.

27. See Ernst Bizer, *Studien zur Geschichte des Abendmahlsstreits im sechzehnten Jahrhundert* (Darmstadt: Wissenschaftliche Buchgemeinschaft, 1962 repr. of the 1940 edition), chap. 1.

28. Hans Asmussen, Helmut Gollwitzer, Friedrich Wilhelm Hopf, Ernst Käsemann, Wilhelm Niesel, Ernst Wolf, *Abendmahlsgemeinschaft?* (Beinheft 3 zur Evangelischen Theologie; Munich: Kaiser, 1937), pp. 198-200.

29. *Zur Lehre vom Hl. Abendmahl: Bericht über das Abendmahlsgespräch der EKD 1947-1957 und Erläuterungen seiner Ergebnisse* (Munich: Kaiser, 2nd ed., 1959); *Lehrgespräch über das Hl. Abendmahl: Stimmen und Studien zu den Arnoldshainer Thesen der Kommission für das Abendmahlsgespräch der EKD* (Munich: Kaiser, 1961). An English text of the Theses may be found in *Scottish Journal of Theology* 15, (1962) 1-3, and *Lutheran Quarterly* 11 (1959): 108-111.

30. *Luther: Lectures on Romans*, Wilhelm Pauck, ed., Library of Christian Classics, 15 (Philadelphia: Westminster Press, 1961), p. 253.

31. *Calvin: Institutes of the Christian Religion* III.21.4; J. T. McNeill, ed., F.L. Battles, tr., Library of Christian Classics, 21 (Philadelphia: Westminster Press, 1960), p. 925.

32. On Beza, see John S. Bray, *Theodore of Beza's Doctrine of Predestination*, Bibliotheca humanistica et reformatorica, 12 (Nieuwkoop: De Graaf, 1975); on Zanchi: Otto Gründler, *Die Gotteslehre*

Girolamo Zanchis und ihre Bedeutung für seine Lehre von der Prä-
destination (Beiträge zur Geschichte und Lehre der reformierten
Kirche, 20; Neukirchen: Neukirchener Verlag, 1965).
33. Lienhard, "Die Verwerfung" (above, note 25), p. 141.
34. *Documents of Lutheran Unity in America*, Richard C. Wolf, ed.
(Philadelphia: Fortress Press, 1966), pp. 198-206.
35. *Book of Confessions* (6.191-193).
36. *The Doctrine of Reprobation in the Christian Reformed Church*, Harry
Boer, (Grand Rapids: Eerdmans, 1983).
37. The publications are cited in note 13.
38. *Konkordie und Kirchengemeinschaft* (see above, note 13), pp. 39-
43; 49-51.
39. Ibid., p. 41.
40. Ibid., p. 50.
41. The term "full communion" plays an important role in the
section on "Goals and Stages" of the ELCA statement, "Ecumenism: The Vision of the ELCA": cf. *A Commentary . . .* (above,
note 10), pp. 90 and 91-97, and Appendix 3: "The Phrase 'Full
Communion' as a Statement of the Ecumenical Goal as Described in the Proposed Ecumenical Policy Statement of the
ELCA: A Dossier Prepared by Michael Root," pp. 142-153.
42. Some options are mentioned in *An Invitation to Action*, pp. 5-
6, d.(5)-(9).
43. Such dialogue may focus on such matters as creation, the Trinity, the doctrine of the Holy Spirit, Scripture and scriptural
hermeneutics, ecclesiology, ministry, church, and world.

REFORMED HERITAGE AND LUTHERAN CONNECTIONS IN THE LIFE OF THE UCC

Representative governance in national and regional judicatories
and a vigorous commitment to social witness, mission outreach,
and ecclesial reform, along with respect for historic creeds and
confessions carry forward the Reformed heritage of the UCC. The
Church is an active member of the World Alliance of Reformed
Churches through delegates elected by the General Synod, one of
whom served recently as vice-president of the Alliance. This membership requires a "position in faith . . . in general agreement with
that of the historic Reformed confessions. . . . "The UCC joined
for a period with the Presbyterian Church in the publication of a
common journal and shares with that church a strong commitment

to the Consultation on Church Union and other ecumenical ventures.

The UCC has been an active participant in the North American Lutheran-Reformed Dialogue since its inception in 1962 and in the Lutheran-Reformed Conversations after the formation of the ELCA in 1988. Its participation was preceded by a day-long New York Consultation in October of 1987 at which UCC and Lutheran (ALC, LCA, LCMS) theologians presented papers on the confessional nature, polity, and teaching on justification of their respective traditions with UPC(USA) and RCA representatives in attendance.

Within the Reformed family, the United Church of Christ has an unusual kinship with Lutheran churches by virtue of its continental Evangelical lineage and its association with historic union churches on both sides of the Atlantic:

1. On May 18 and June 15, 1980, the German *Evangelische Kirche der Union* (EKU/DDR and EKU/BRD), consummating a twenty-year relationship, voted to enter *Kirchengemeinschaft* (church fellowship) with the United Church of Christ. A reciprocal resolution was passed by the General Synod of the UCC in June 1981. Since that time, the participating churches have been active in implementing full communion through mutual exchange on concerns of theology and mission.

2. For 250 years congregations of Reformed and Lutheran heritage in Pennsylvania and Maryland have shared the same church facilities as well as many common activities. Along with the strong present desire to establish independent facilities, a process of self-examination has been undertaken regarding the mutual recognition of pastoral ministry and eucharistic practice among the partner churches. The document "Recognition of Ministry in Union Churches," prepared after a four-year study by Lutheran and UCC pastors in such union churches, states: "We celebrate the 'union church' as a grassroots ecumenical opportunity for the laity and clergy of our two traditions to learn to live together in harmony and Christian unity. . . . We urge serious consideration of the 'Joint Statement on Ministry' contained in *An Invitation to Action*. Our experience as union church pastors has shown that 'there are no substantive matters concerning ministry which should divide us.' . . . We recommend that clergy and laity of union churches engage in shared worship, ministry, education, programming, and administration to the greatest extent possible under local conditions." In addition, guidelines are offered "governing the practice of eucharistic fellowship," including the recommendation of a

shared eucharist "on ecumenical occasions such as Worldwide Communion Sunday."

In its official response to *An Invitation to Action* in 1989, the 17th General Synod recognized the partners in the Lutheran-Reformed Dialogue "as churches in which the Gospel is proclaimed and the sacraments administered according to the ordinance of Christ," and their ordained ministries to be "both valid and effective." The resolution looked "forward to the day when 'church fellowship' can be fully embraced by, and implemented among, each of the partners in this dialogue."

The Church and Ministry Committees of the Associations (i.e., regional subdivisions within the 39 Conferences of the UCC), as the immediate gateways to pastoral ministry in the United Church, implement and interpret General Synod actions on ministry. Clergy from other denominations are reviewed by these committees on matters of theology and practice, and action on ministerial standing is taken accordingly.

As in other churches in which polity or historical development affects the status of inherited confessions, it is churchwide "traditions" that become doctrinal indicators of the church's theology. Recognizing this dynamic, the Leuenberg declaration of full communion between Lutheran and Reformed churches speaks of "confessions *and* traditions" that define participating churches, and confessional equivalencies are recognized in Anglican liturgies in the Lutheran-Episcopal Dialogue. In the UCC, in addition to the constitutional documents, textual carriers and shapers of its theological tradition are to be found in its corporate statements of faith and mission, in patterns of worship, hymnody, catechetical and confirmation materials, and standard for ordination. At a less official level, movements for theological self-definition have played an important part in clarifying UCC doctrinal identity in recent years. Influential documents in the formation of the theological ethos in the UCC are the following:

1. Official Texts:

a. The United Church's *Statement of Faith*, universally used (in its traditional or doxological form) in local, regional, and national church gatherings, and widely used by congregations in worship and church covenants. The *Statement* was approved at the Second General Synod as a faithful rendition of the confession of faith in the *Basis of Union* of the uniting denominations.

b. The UCC Constitution and Bylaws stipulated that the uniting denominations join "without break in their respective continuities and traditions. Thus the "creeds and platforms of Congregationalism"—the title of the 1893 compilation by Williston Walker that includes the Cambridge Platform and Savoy Declaration with the Westminster Confession, the 1865 Burial Hill Declaration and the Creed of 1883, but not the later Kansas City statement of faith—and the confessional symbols of the Evangelical and Reformed Church—Heidelberg Catechism, Augsburg Confession, and Luther's Small Catechism—continue to be resources for interpreting UCC theological identity as formulated in the Constitution, the Basis of Union, and the Statement of Faith. This historic confessional and creedal tradition is given high visibility in current UCC ventures in self-awareness, e.g., the volumes of the UCC *Living Theological Heritage* series and the *Craigville Colloquies*, mentioned below.

c. The UCC *Book of Worship*, approved by General Synod after extensive testing in congregations, used consistently by Conferences, Associations, and the General Synod for worship services, sacraments, and rites of the Church, and widely used by UCC clergy for the same purposes.

d. The United Church of Christ *Hymnal* and the predecessor churches' *Pilgrim Hymnal* and *Evangelical and Reformed Hymnal*, all containing earlier order for the sacraments, rites, and other worship services. A new hymnal is now in the early planning stage.

e. The *Manual on Ministry*, prepared by the UCC Office for Church Life and Leadership, with procedures for the ordination and commissioning of ministers, universally used by judicatories responsible for the ordering of ministry.

f. Two confirmation series produced by the Christian Education Agency, and a volume, *My Confirmation*, that has enjoyed wide use for a long time in conjunction with other catechetical material (primarily the Heidelberg Catechism, but also the Evangelical Catechism) where it is employed.

g. The theological lore developing through actions taken by General Synod on specific theological issues, e.g., responses to BEM, *An Invitation to Action*, COCU, through resolutions prepared and churchwide studies executed by the Church's Council on Ecumenism, and on general issues of mission and service with their theological preambles.

h. The "Statement on Mission" growing out of a national conference on the UCC's theology of mission in January 1987, where the agencies of the Church and a cross-section of its membership were represented.

2. Unofficial Texts, Growing out of Theological Initiatives in the UCC:

a. under the auspices of agencies or working groups of the Church:

1. Board of Homeland Ministries, "Statement of Commitment" (1972); a declaration on the theology of evangelism by participants at a Deering, N.H., conference that became the basis for UCC evangelism programs.

2. Office of Church Life and Leadership Task Force, "Sound Teaching in the United Church of Christ" (1977), a statement used in the conversations between the EKU and the UCC.

3. Office of Church Life and Leadership Task Force, "Theology in the United Church of Christ" (1986), a commentary on the need for theological inquiry in the UCC.

4. EKU/UCC Working Group papers on controverted theological issues, 1985-86.

5. Board for Homeland Ministries, "Living Theological Heritage" project, since 1988; seven volumes of documents that have shaped the UCC's theological tradition (ecumenical creeds; patristic and medieval writings; Reformation confessions, catechisms, and writings of reformers; platforms, covenants, declarations and writings of the New England tradition; documents from Reformed and Evangelical traditions of the eighteenth and nineteenth centuries; Mercersburg theology; missionary traditions and documents from the eighteenth and nineteenth centuries; documents of ethnic traditions in the UCC—Hungarian, Volga German, native American, Asian American, Hawaiian, Samoan; nineteenth and twentieth-century Congregational creeds and confessions; theological texts of the UCC since 1957; texts of current theological ferment).

b. grass roots texts:

1. Biblical-Theological-Liturgical Group (1979), "East Petersburg Declaration," protesting accommodation to culture and affirming biblical authority and the christological center.

2. Biblical Witness Fellowship (1983), "Dubuque Declaration" pleading for traditional doctrinal standards and an infallibilist reading of Scripture; it became the basis for the BWF evangelical caucus within the UCC.

3. UCC seminary teacher (group of the "Seminary 39"), "A Most Difficult and Urgent Time" (1983), a widely circulated statement challenging cultural accommodation in the church and calling for biblical and theological integrity.

4. Witness Statements 1-7 of the *Craigville Colloquies*, 1984-1990, on: The Confessional Nature of the UCC; The Authority of Scripture; Baptism; Eucharist; Ministry; Abortion; Justification and Justice. The Colloquies gather UCC clergy and laity, exploring controversial questions and drafting consensus statements with wide media coverage.

5. Christians for Justice Action (1985), "The Prophet Speaks to Our Times," a statement warning of the danger of a privatistic faith and affirming the link between theological renewal and social action; it has become the basis for the CJA caucus in the UCC.

6. Statements and literature on theological renewal by newly formed groups such as the Mercersburg Society, the Order of Corpus Christi, the Charismatic Fellowship, and the Spirituality Network.

By polity, history, and heritage, the United Church of Christ has been open to the challenges and forces of its social context. With this openness came a susceptibility to cultural accommodation. It is no accident that one of its major theologians, H. Richard Niebuhr, wrote a definitive study on *Christ and Culture*. Halfway through its short life the Church began to recognize both the dangers and opportunities of its life "on the boundary" and determined to reassert its theological identity while maintaining its contextual commitments, especially to "the struggle for justice and peace" (Statement of Faith). The renewed awareness of its confessional and covenantal heritage and the theological ferment manifest in the movements and documents cited above represent both the recovery of its roots and the intention "in each generation to make this faith its own..." (Constitution of the UCC, Preamble). The UCC is a laboratory of learning how to live committed to classical texts as they speak the word to contemporary contexts. As such, it is willing to walk with other churches faithful to the word and engaged with the world.

List of Participants

REFORMED CHURCH IN AMERICA

Paul Fries, New Brunswick, New Jersey
Lynn Japinga, Kentwood, Michigan
Douglas W. Fromm, Jr., Ridgewood, New Jersey (staff)

PRESBYTERIAN CHURCH (USA)

Aurelia T. Fule, Louisville, Kentucky
Keith Nickle, Pittsburgh, Pennsylvania (co-chair)
Margrethe B. J. Brown, Rochester, New York (staff)

UNITED CHURCH OF CHRIST

Gabriel Fackre, Newton, Massachusetts
Elizabeth Nordbeck, Newton, Massachusetts
John Thomas, Cleveland, Ohio (staff since 1992)

Evangelical Lutheran Church in America

Karlfried Froehlich, Princeton, New Jersey
Mary B. Havens, Columbia, South Carolina
(1988-1991 member and co-chair)
Timothy F. Lull, Berkeley, California (co-chair)
Robin Mattison, Philadelphia, Pennsylvania
Ronald F. Thiemann, Cambridge, Massachusetts
David L. Tiede, St. Paul, Minnesota
Daniel F. Martensen, Chicago, Illinois (staff)
William G. Rusch, Chicago, Illinois (staff, part-time)

A COMMON DISCOVERY:
LEARNING ABOUT THE CHURCHES OF THE REFORMATION IN NORTH AMERICA TODAY

This study guide for congregations is designed to help Lutherans and members of the Reformed tradition discover what they have in common and where they differ in their understandings of baptism, eucharist, and ministry. The implications of those learnings for mission and ecumenism are explored. Each of the seven sessions contains a vignette, questions, and background notes from each of the two traditions. Resource materials are also listed. At the end of each session there are study helps for exploring sections of *A Common Calling* that relate to the session theme. Those helps include questions and a brief commentary.

A Common Discovery will be of special interest to members of the Evangelical Lutheran Church in America and three churches in the Reformed tradition, the Presbyterian Church USA, the Reformed Church in America, and the United Church of Christ. As these churches prepare to make a decision about the proposal for "full communion," this study guide may help their congregations explore how approving the recommendations in *A Common Calling* could affect their lives.

Copies of *A Common Discovery* (code 69-2318) may be purchased from the Evangelical Lutheran Church in America Distribution Service. To order call 1-800-328-4648.

Also available from Augsburg:

Rusch, William G. and Martensen, Daniel F. *The Leuenberg Agreement and Lutheran-Reformed Relationships: Evaluations by the North American and European Theologians.* 1989 (code 9-2436).

Rusch, William G. *A Commentary on "Ecumenism: The Vision of the ELCA."* 1990 (code 9-2515).